LITTLE KIDS
BiG CITY

LITTLE KIDS
B*I*G CITY

Tales From a Real House in New York City

With Lessons on Life and Love for Your Own
Concrete Jungle

BY ALEX McCORD
& SIMON VAN KEMPEN

STERLING & ROSS PUBLISHERS
NEW YORK

Published by
Sterling & Ross Publishers
New York, NY 10001
www.sterlingandross.com

For bulk or special sales contact sales@sterlingandross.com.

Library of Congress Cataloging-in-Publication Data
McCord, Alex.
Little kids, big city : tales from a real house in New York City (with lessons
on life and love for your own concrete jungle) / by Alex McCord and Simon
van Kempen.
p. cm.
ISBN 978-0-9821392-2-6 (pbk.)
1. Parenthood--New York (State)--New York. 2. Child rearing--New York
(State)--New York. I. Van Kempen, Simon. II. Title.
HQ755.8M414 2010
306.874092--dc22
[B]
2010005899

Photo on page 208: Edward "Garou" Linders
Cover design: The Book Designers
Book design: Rachel Trusheim

10 9 8 7 6 5 4 3 2 1

Printed in the United States of America.

To the Chums,
François & Johan,
without whom this book would not have been possible

To our Mothers,
Elaine van Kempen & Alexis Williams,
without whom this book would also not have been possible

and

To the Memory of
François Johan Walter "Frank" van Kempen &
David Robert "Bob" McCord,
because they had quite a bit to do with it, too…

Table of Contents

Introduction

Alex

I moved to New York City in 1996 after having spent a couple of fashionably nomadic years running around Europe modeling, acting and drinking cappuccino in the morning and champagne in the evening. I rode in yellow Porsches with cute boys whose mothers' homes were photographed for magazines, read *The Economist* and *Mother Jones* for balance and all I wanted to do was act, make beautiful things and live large. Pursuing dual careers as an actress and graphic designer, I had no intention of even choosing a steady relationship, let alone getting married. I never wanted to settle down, because to me it meant succumbing to all the things I didn't want in my life. I was afraid of waking up one day with a boring job, a marriage to someone I didn't particularly like who was the best person available at the time, a minivan and a house that looked like everyone else's. I did all those things our mothers warned us about and had fun doing them. Along the way I met a crazy Australian who was in town for three weeks on business, and at the time, an alliance with a "use-by date" was a good thing. Don't things happen when you least expect them? A year later we were married.

One thing that's completely consistent about my life is that I've always been quick to recognize something I want when I see it, and I wanted Simon. My family was a bit shell-shocked not only when I announced that I planned to get married, but also that I chose a man everyone agreed my father would have loved. We were wildly in love then and still are to this day.

Engaged!

Simon

In February 1999, I moved to Sydney after spending 13 years living in London, to act as a luxury hotel consultant and expand the company's Asia-Pacific business. In May I was sent to see a potential client in New York, and very early one morning, severely jet-lagged, I logged on to a dating website that I'd joined in Australia. I temporarily changed my location to NYC, as I was only planning on being in town for three weeks and wasn't seeking the woman of my dreams: merely a drink, a dinner and a local's perspective on the Big Apple. I remember seeing that a new profile "Yetisrule" had just appeared and seemed to be in the process of joining the site. That early in the morning I really didn't expect to find anyone else logged on, but then again I was in the city that never sleeps. Little did I know then that if I met this *Yeti Who Rules*, I would embark on a journey that 10 and a half years later has brought me to be sitting here writing on the Acela train as I dash between NYC and Washington, D.C. But what's more surprising is that that early Sunday morning jet lag set off a chain of events that had me moving back to the northern hemisphere, disappointing my mum in the process and marrying a woman who I never really believed existed for me.

For the next nine months I lived out of a suitcase, as every month I would visit my four main clients, each on a different continent. Given my itinerant lifestyle—and I was now madly in love with Alex—I decided to move base camp from Sydney to New York, which basically involved putting everything back in a shipping container that the year prior had been shipped from London to Australia. Alex and I put down digs in a duplex apartment on the Upper West Side of Manhattan, after she happily scrambled out of her rent-stabilized but dreary one bedroom on the Upper East Side. We were married at Maxim's, the Madison and 61st Street sister of the iconic Parisian restaurant.

Alex & Simon Get Married!

IV

Alex

We continued as newlyweds in our two-bedroom apartment on the UWS, and took on the world as a team. Simon flew around the world consulting (occasionally I joined him if his hotel clients needed a graphic designer), while I happily acted, designed, noodled around with the stock market and threw parties for our friends. We traveled to China, Europe, Australia and wherever work or whimsy took us. After 18 months in our rental apartment we decided that the time was right to buy a place.

When two people get together to buy a home, it's a big deal for both. We each had our own ideas of what the perfect apartment looked like, but soon realized our deal breakers were pretty similar. We both wanted outdoor space—just living near a park wasn't going to cut it. We nearly made an offer on a quirky little pre-war one bedroom on Jane Street in Greenwich Village, but the triangular terrace only got direct sunlight for one hour a day. Not good enough. After a month or so of looking, we found a co-op triplex in Park Slope, a lovely area in Brooklyn, with a sixth floor terrace from which we could see a spectacular view of Manhattan, New Jersey and even Staten Island if you looked around the corner.

We settled in and began making the apartment our own, including a gut renovation, though we still hadn't changed our minds about children—we didn't want any and were sticking to it. So we said. As the next two and a half years went by and our relationship got stronger we did gradually change our minds. Maybe there was a reason we'd bought a three-bedroom apartment after all. The best way I can describe it is that we wanted to share our love or perhaps our love had grown so much that there was now more to share. I remember at one point, the cat Simon owned with his first wife was run over by a car in London and we both got really emotional. Sometime after that we noticed for the first time we were both having clucky feelings. I looked at babies on the streets of New York and for the first time, I could imagine myself having one. Somewhere around Halloween we agreed that I'd toss the pills, and by February I'd almost forgotten we'd done that when I threw up in Times Square. At 8:30 in the morning. Not hungover.

With me pregnant, we threw ourselves full tilt into preparation for our life change. I didn't know what parenthood was going to look like, but had no intention of leaving the city or even changing our lifestyle much beyond welcoming the new member of the family. I had no idea of the changes in store, and (let's not kid ourselves) there have been quite a few. I'm happy, however, to report that it's possible to be a parent and *not* get stuck in a boring job and relationship, with a boring car and house. It *is* possible to have children and not feel as though you've "settled." You *can* be eight months pregnant and wear a leather miniskirt. You *can* take a baby on the subway, to a museum or to Africa. Call me naïve, but I didn't expect that. I'm still me, and I still love the city. Now I get to share that experience with my two adorable, sassy, frustrating but mind-blowingly loved boys.

Once they were born, I couldn't believe how often I would find myself either laughing or crying. I had no idea of the indignities that parents of young children deal with, both from their own offspring and the holier-than-thou people who always have an opinion about the quality of one's parenting. I began to write things down in 2004 when François was just a few months old. Initially these stories were just for him to keep and laugh at later, and I kept it up when Johan arrived two years later. Fast-forward a few more years to a time when I had the opportunity to put it all together in a book, and here we are. I hope that when you read this book, if you are like I once was, adamantly single and childless by choice, that you'll see you can become a parent without losing yourself. Your sanity is another matter, but we'll get to that later. No one is a good parent all the time—nor is anyone a bad parent all the time. Anyone who tries to say they are is lying to themselves. If you're in love and thinking of having kids, here's a taste of what's to come. If you've already had yours, I hope you'll laugh either with us or at our exploits.

Simon
For three years Alex and I lived only for ourselves and had an amazing time doing it, but as my clock ticked ever closer to my 40th birthday I began to feel like our union and our intense love needed to be shared. Soon after François and then Johan were born, they made us both richer and rounder as people and as parents.

Nothing can prepare you for having children other than one's innate instinct. However as Alex and I both found, reading others' experiences made us realize that we weren't too far off track with how we adjusted to parenthood. There probably is nothing more rewarding than watching life bloom and six years in, each day brings surprises, some magical and some less so. If you take nothing away but a wry smile after reading our little tome, then we've done our job. This is not some how-to book by experts but simply a take on what we've discovered along the way by having two little kids in a great big city, and what a GREAT city NYC is.

WELCOME TO OUR WORLD:
A PRIMER ON PARENTHOOD

6:15 a.m. – Awaken to a kick in the face. Sleepily remember that a six-year-old boy crawled into our bed at some unknowable hour. Think he is ours but can't be sure until looking. Open eyes. Yes, that's François. Sigh as he begs for a "bouncy train ride" on Dad's legs as the cat attacks his stuffed shark, complete with hissing and growling. "Cats don't eat sharks," Simon whispers as we all try to untangle the mess.

6:30 a.m. – After fielding repeated entreaties for ice cream(?) and brightly delivered interrogations ("Why are you still sleeping? I'm awake!"), stumble out of bed with François, noting that Simon has rolled over and gone back into a mild coma. Explain why a shoulder ride up the stairs is not a good idea this early. Pour freshly squeezed OJ and high fiber organic cereal for child and turn on espresso machine. Try not to die while it heats up.

6:45 a.m. – With caffeine, outlook begins to improve. Welcome four-year-old son Johan as he sleepily trudges out of his bedroom, on the hunt for his egg-shaped whisk with which he is intent on making pancakes. Find whisk, make just enough batter for one or two pancakes each. Allow two happy boys to flip pancakes. Pull another latte.

7:15 a.m. – Hear rather large feet hitting the floor downstairs; turn on kettle for Simon. French press is ready as he appears. Discuss varying experiences during the night—being pounced on by cats and children. Recall hearing the cat being sick during the night. Examine bottoms of feet for traces of cat vomit; none found. Remind Simon of the deal forged years ago: Alex takes care of poo and Simon is in charge of vomit. Leave pancake-eaters in care of husband with a proclamation that the crayons don't come out unless everyone is completely dressed and ready to leave. Hit the shower.

7:45 a.m. – Dressed and ready, trade places with husband and begin making school lunch and snacks. Slice homemade bread, look for organic peanut butter (discovered inside the lobster pot in the oven). Pack lunch into François' backpack. Ensure various bits are in order: karate uniform, signed permission slip for aquarium trip, etc. Ooh, aquarium, reminds me to feed the fish. Yes, I have parental ADD.

8:00 a.m. – Suddenly recall Johan needs a crazy hat for Crazy Hat Day at pre-K. Find a cloth box in playroom, create a hat with strategically placed scissor slices. Result is actually better than if we'd spent loads of time on it; feel (perhaps unwarranted) pride in this. Johan is thrilled. Simon finds the offending cat vomit and cleans up.

8:15 a.m. – Nanny Coleen arrives to take Johan for a morning walk before pre-K starts. Simon and François leave for school; I head downstairs to my home office for another day of madness, ahem, work.

Chapter 1

Does a German Shepherd Need a Birth Plan?

Why Childbirth is Not an Intellectual Activity

Simon

When Alex and I first fell in love and decided to marry, children were definitely not on our agenda. However as time wore on, and with me then in my late 30s with my 40th approaching, my mind started to wonder if fatherhood was something I sought.

I had been born to a 50-year-old father who unfortunately had died before I realized that he was somewhat "old" to be my dad (this was in the early '60s when most parents of newborns were under 30). And so if I was going to parent children I wanted to be young enough to see them through college and, more importantly, be able to run around the backyard with them without the aid of a walking stick.

Remarkably 10 years on, Alex and I are still as attuned today as we were then. I remember rapidly broaching this with Alex not more than 24 hours after the thought entered my head and delightfully and simultaneously she'd been thinking the same thing. Our love was strong, we'd had a ball living the DINKY (Double Income No Kids Yet) life and now almost four years into our relationship, parenthood was beckoning. In October 2002 Alex stopped taking the pill and within four months she was pregnant (or using the now common vernacular, *we* were pregnant!) and our life was about to change, more than we ever thought it would.

Alex
The best way to describe our change of heart about kids is that our love grew, and we thought we might want to share it. While my mother had counseled me not to have a baby unless I couldn't sleep at night because I wanted one so desperately, I knew I'd never get to that point. I do, however, remember clearly thinking, "If I've become ambivalent, may as well try and see what happens. We'll never be *more* ready than this." When I look back on that time and think that these two kids might not be here, I'm so happy we changed our minds.

At the time I became pregnant with François in 2003, we had been going to a family practice doctor whose pregnancy and childbirth expertise finished at pap smears. When the little double line showed up on the pregnancy test, I called her and she directed me to Dr. Blank (yes, that was his name!), a rather dour obstetrician whose first line to me after his nurse had me take another test was, "So, do you want to keep it?" He went down a list of his requirements for birthing mothers, including "when to decide on a c-section," and by the end of the 15 minutes we both knew quite well that we'd never see each other again.

Simon

The meeting with Dr. Blank was the only significant appointment I missed for either birth. In the early stages of pregnancy it seems at least for the man a pretty abstract phenomenon—sure, I'd been there for conception, but now, at least initially, I was a bit player as the embryo grew both in size and significance. After missing the initial appointment I was determined to be with Alex and the then nameless embryo for every step of the way.

Alex

My next appointment was with a female OB in Park Slope, home of the ParkSlopeParents.com message board made famous in 2007 with a so-ridiculous-it-got-headlines discussion on gender-specific baby hats and where feminism can be taken to extremes. This OB lost me as a client (the word patient doesn't seem right here), however, when she stated that insertion of an IV was a deal-breaking requirement and refused to ask for my permission before performing an episiotomy. Not only would she not agree to ask first, but she seemed surprised that I even knew what it was and that I would question her absolute authority to perform one. Sorry, but I'm not interested in being sliced and diced against my will. Also, because my blood type was negative, she immediately wrote in my chart that I needed RhoGAM, an "antidote" that can be administered to a mother if the father's blood is positive. Turns out Simon and I are both negative, something that only happens in 4 percent of all pregnancies. The doctor just assumed that it wasn't possible for us to both be negative, and looked at me funny when I stated that if I didn't need medication, I didn't want it. Don't get me started on the vagaries of our 21st-century health care system and its lack of support for mothers, or that intervention-free natural childbirth is barely tolerated by the medical establishment because the timing can't be controlled and it doesn't make the hospital or the providers any money.

Simon
While with the Park Slope OB-GYN, we had the first sonogram and saw the little blip on the screen—our child-to-be. They say seeing is believing and as nothing was happening inside *me*, seeing confirmation on the video monitor that indeed my spermatozoa had penetrated and infiltrated one of Alex's ova made me aware that my days as a footloose and fancy-free guy might be coming to an end.

Alex
I received a letter yesterday from an organization dedicated to preserving mother's rights in New York City, and it sort of made me want to grab a big banner and start marching through the streets screaming. The stats they quoted referenced a 40 percent cesarean section rate in the city, and I wonder how can that be acceptable? Are we heading toward

Brave New World, where babies are scientifically created in petri dishes and gestated in artificial wombs? Oh wait, we're already there. Are we heading toward a *Wall-E* existence, where we ride around in carts everywhere and do nothing for ourselves so that our bodies break down and we're all fat, oozy blobs drinking protein from a straw? Somebody slap me, please!!!

Not everyone will agree with me. This is one area where I veer toward the radical. Ideally I'd like to have had my babies at home and didn't only because my midwife wasn't covered for home births by her insurance. If I say much more about insurance, I'll give myself a headache. Modern medicine is great if there's a problem—a difficult pregnancy, trouble conceiving, etc. But if you're a healthy woman with a trouble-free pregnancy, there is usually no reason why you can't give birth with a minimum of fuss and bother. It really, really irritates me that women feel forced to give away their power, and allow themselves to be swayed by the medical community's opinion and convenience when it comes to a hugely significant event in their lives. If you open up *What to Expect When You're Expecting*, which I feel should be renamed *What to Have Nightmares About When You're Expecting*, you see over and over again, "If your practitioner permits," "You're doctor will advise you," "Balance your wishes with what is acceptable" and all that rot. Make no mistake, there are problematic pregnancies and high-risk pregnancies where high-level medical involvement is essential; I'm not talking about those. A normal pregnancy is not a disease, and I absolutely hate it that many people treat it as such. My only experience of pregnancy and childbirth has been in New York, a highly urban area, and I wonder if there's a little more hysteria about the process and desire to micromanage it here. My theory is that people who are type A and perhaps more highly strung in general can swing toward wanting assistance, outsourcing and problem solving, sometimes when there is no problem to be solved. In my experience, there is also a tendency among urbanites to want to be at the forefront of whatever advances technology or medicine make. I remember when the 3-D ultrasound technology became available, many local people I knew started jumping on it. Just because the best and the brightest doctors may be in urban areas, doesn't mean we need to call upon them unless there's a danger to the mom or baby.

Throughout the first few months of pregnancy with our eldest, I read everything I could get my hands on— from Sheila Kitzinger to *Spiritual Midwifery*. I began to understand the anger women felt by having the control of the birthing process ripped from their hands, and hey baby, I'm a control freak. Though I grew frustrated, I didn't think there was much to be solved by simply becoming angry (à la Naomi Wolfe's rant on her experiences of childbirth). Surely there had to be a better way. I found it in the idea of natural, midwife-assisted childbirth, something that I had never had cause to think of before. I never planned to be a natural birth advocate, but the process really made sense to me. Use modern medicine to make sure that there's nothing abnormal going on with the pregnancy, then when the time comes, let nature take its course. The midwives we found had definite rules, such as not letting a pregnancy go more than two weeks overdue and a list of conditions like diabetes and placenta previa that ruled out the attempt, but beyond that, it was pretty much anything goes. I never felt the need to establish a birth plan with my rules, because we were all in agreement. No drugs, lots of food and drink before, during and after, plus good music and plenty of support.

Once I made the decision to go natural, I wanted to give myself the best possible chance to succeed, and thought, what do you do if you're going to put your body through a huge physical ordeal? You work out and you train. Prior to becoming pregnant with François I had topped the scales at my heaviest weight ever, about 130 pounds. At 5'8" that still wasn't too shabby but more than I was used to or comfortable with, and the day I knew something had to give was when I met up with a college friend who exclaimed, "Alex, you're zaftig and I like it!" It was said as a compliment (I think), but to someone who thought of herself as young and svelte, it was not what I wanted to hear. Simon was also getting up there on the weight chart; with no children and relatively sedentary jobs, we'd settled into a life of entertaining regularly and going out for delightful tasting menus at fabulous restaurants with wine pairings and desserts. I've always said I'll eat anything that doesn't eat me first, and without a regular exercise plan that was a recipe for larger sizes and muffin tops. Oops. My pregnancy gave us both a wakeup call and we were able to undo the damage pretty easily. We hired a trainer who had worked with a couple of pregnant women before, and got him to work us each out three times per week. In effect I

7

was training for the birth, just as you'd train for a marathon. We joked that I was training for the extreme sport of natural childbirth. Deep squats, hand weights, leg lifts and treadmill speed-walking ensued for six months, and continued up to the week of my due date.

Alex, Pregnant

People often ask me what my secret is for maintaining

a slim body after two babies, and I usually say that there is no secret, though if there were I'd write a diet book and call it *Mama-So-Thin* or something terribly catchy, make millions and retire to St. Barths. Good genes play a big part— everyone on both sides of my family is tall and skinny. However, I'm a firm believer in using whatever excuse you need to in order to eliminate bad habits, and going into the childbearing years I did have a few. Having gone to school in the Midwest, I had fallen into the trap so many do and become addicted to fast food, soda and junk treats. I used my pregnancies as an opportunity to kick those addictions. It didn't happen overnight. I had pretty nasty morning sickness with François through the first and even into the second trimester, and the only thing that would settle my stomach in the morning was a sausage biscuit and hash browns from McDonalds. This was the one time in our lives together that Simon even teased me about being "so American," with my Coke and my McDonalds. Once I stopped getting sick, however, I started to crave spinach, and recognized that I had a real opportunity. Shortly after the morning sickness wore off, I lost my taste for soda and vowed not to let it come back. I immediately started drinking sparkling mineral water like Perrier or Pellegrino to replace the bubbles, and allowed myself plain chocolate if I needed a sweet fix. I replaced the caffeine with lattes and cappuccinos, although during pregnancy I had one a day, not three. When I wanted to have a drink, I did, and would drink half a glass of wine or champagne. My opinion is that women should take good care of themselves while pregnant, so that they feel positive and feel well. While I wouldn't recommend keeping up a drug habit or smoking, I made the choice to have wine when I felt like it, dye my hair and eat whatever I wanted within reason. I did research to see whether the most extreme admonitions, such as swearing off caffeine, alcohol, hair dye, mayonnaise, etc., really seemed to be valid, and after reading up on them decided that moderation was key. Throughout my pregnancy I gave in to any craving I felt, such as the spinach and others that popped up like scrambled eggs, veggie pizza and raisins. If I had suddenly craved chalk, ecstasy or Elmer's Glue, I'd have thought twice, but I reckon in the long run eating too many supersize value meals will cause many more long-term health problems than a nice glass of Burgundy when you want it.

Even after I was no longer racing to work in the morning with a barf bag, I still got really terrible motion sickness, and anyone who has taken a taxi through stop-and-go traffic can relate. I swore off cabs for the rest of the pregnancy, and even insisted on taking the subway home after a couple of late nights out. The last thing I wanted to do was have a nice dinner and then lose it on the way home. I really hate throwing up—wow, that's profound, eh? I don't think I know anyone who *likes* vomiting. Anyway, one of the great things about being pregnant is that people assume you're crazy, so I was able to entertain myself by yelling at overzealous taxi drivers before giving up riding in cabs altogether.

All along the way during both pregnancies, but especially the first as everything was such a new experience, I kept thinking, "What is the big deal?!" People constantly asked me if I was OK and gave me the hairy eyeball if I dared to order anything on the pregnancy watch list such as wine, soft cheese or sushi, and once I almost got myself thrown off a plane. On the way home from St. Barths we hadn't been able to get a direct flight from St. Martin and took a 20-seater to San Juan, Puerto Rico. A very short, very large flight attendant made a huge deal about me sitting in an exit row at six-and-a-bit-months along. She insisted I wouldn't be able to open the door. I knew good and well I could open it much more easily than she could, and asked her if she'd like me to demonstrate. She didn't like that. Simon stood in the background snickering, and only intervened when I started yelling and he didn't want me to be removed from the flight and wind up in airport jail. It just really bothered me that people assumed pregnancy is a debilitating condition, when it isn't. If anything, that care should be applied to new moms, who are often so worn out they can barely function.

Simon
We'd discussed and agreed that neither of us wanted to know the sex of the fetus. By the time of the next sonogram and knowing that now at 20 weeks it was possible for the technician to ascertain its sex, we told him to tell us everything else he saw throughout the sonogram but nothing that would indicate its gender. As Alex was lying on the bench, with goo all over her swollen belly, and he moved the "thing" over her skin, he suddenly had a short

11

sharp breath that indicated to us that something was awry. Our eyes darted and interlocked and I, somewhat tepidly, asked him what was the matter. He paused, then let out a little laugh but said nothing to comfort what by now were two confused and concerned parents-to-be. He broke this speechless segment with comforting words; everything was fine. Alex and I although a little assured, were wondering exactly what had caused both his and our hearts to skip a beat. He said that any explanation would reveal the gender and we quickly decided that it was more important for us to understand exactly what he'd seen than to remain in the dark. He calmly explained that as he moved the camera around he had been unable to locate both arms. Alex and I breathed a little harder as he stated that the second arm was in an unusual position. Apparently the arm was angled over its body with its fingers tightly clasped around its testicles.

He laughed and so did we.

That was the stage that we discovered that our healthy five-month-old fetus was male and had been busy holding his dangly bits. A boy! Henceforth named François, in honor of my father.

Alex

About six months in with François, the Elizabeth Seton Childbearing Center where I intended to deliver closed due to a huge increase in their insurance premiums, apparently because the center was not located inside a hospital. We were all outraged, and I was disappointed to learn that I'd have to deliver in a hospital. St. Vincent's in Greenwich

Village was willing to take all the existing Seton patients and basically stay out of the way, so we reconciled ourselves to the idea. With natural childbirth, a good midwife knows when medical intervention is needed, and during François' birth, the St. Vincent's crew gave us a room and let us do our thing without unasked-for meddling.

Simon

Fathers can breathe deeply, too. Although dogs mightn't need a birth plan in these touchy-feely times it's almost de rigueur that both parents-to-be attend birthing classes, which encompass the birthing process as well as breast feeding; complete with little plastic dolls to feed. All throughout my schooling as well as subsequent studying as an adult I have often been too impatient to learn from reading books and attending classes. I have always been more of a learn-on-the-job kind of guy and so it was with some reluctance on my part that we attended classes. I firmly believe that humans and in fact all female mammals had been birthing for millennia and that our primeval instinct would assert itself when faced with what is a most natural process. I remember sitting on the floor with my legs crossed and a pillow stuffed up my shirt trying to invoke the feeling of having a pregnant belly and stifling my laughter at the absurdity I felt. From my memory we failed to attend the last couple of classes as by then we both just wanted to let instinct take over when the time came.

Alex

One downside to my laid-back attitude was the fact that I didn't keep regimented track of my periods, so couldn't be 100 percent sure when the last one was prior to conceiving. For that reason we did an early ultrasound, but between that uncertainty and switching providers three times, François' due date was moved up two weeks. We didn't know it at the time, but that would come back to haunt us.

At 7:30 p.m. on October 25, 2003, François was 11 days late and counting. The 14-day mark was approaching, and Simon and I were both becoming worried. That point is normally "game over" for natural childbirth, and I would have to have a synthetic induction. Even for someone with a high pain tolerance like me, the speed at which contractions start during induction usually causes most women to give up on a medication-free delivery. In order to get labor going, I tried everything: from speed-walking up and down the stairs in our triplex to watching *Bowling for Columbine* while drinking castor oil that Simon had thoughtfully prepared in a milkshake. He then (even more thoughtfully) cleaned up the projectile vomit that occurred five minutes later. After trying that twice I opted for drinking it straight, which stayed down and worked. Finally, over a dinner of moules frites and champagne at Belleville in Park Slope, contractions started, and we were ecstatic. We stayed up all night, and since the Rugby World Cup was on, Simon used the counter clock to time the contractions. Twenty-seven hours from the first twinge, François made his entrance.

Baby François with Alexis (Alex's mom)

Although he arrived 12 days late by the calendar, the midwife and nurse agreed that upon examination of the vernix, he wasn't late at all. Apparently that white stuff covering the baby at birth starts to look less like body lotion and more like cottage cheese the later a pregnancy goes, and his was very, very smooth. Who knew? Not me. Evidently the first date was right, but hindsight was 20/20—at least the date snafu didn't interfere with the ability to go natural.

We learned from François' birth not to go to the hospital too early because we didn't want to wait around, which almost caused a commotion with Johan's birth.

One of the best things about natural childbirth was the rush of adrenaline afterwards. Although the final stages of labor were very, very painful, I never used our code word (tin can) for "game over, give me drugs." I definitely recommend using a code word, because it was kind of fun to scream, "I want drugs, give me drugs" through a contraction and have the midwife, nurse and Simon all know I wasn't serious. Once he was finally out of my body, I experienced a tsunami of endorphins that was almost orgasmic, and I understand completely the stories other women have written about ecstatic birth. Simon was sitting behind me at the point of birth, and later when we untangled ourselves he discovered he'd actually ejaculated though hadn't felt any of the normal lead-up to that. It may seem distasteful to some, and definitely neither of us was thinking of sex at the time, but with the rush of emotion and my lower nerve endings going crazy, it's not too far a stretch to say that it's a profound experience. Once François was out and we'd bonded, I passed him to the nurse who did the weighing and the testing and such, while I bounded around the room and through a shower like I'd just won a race, and Simon ordered pizza so that we didn't have to experience the joys of hospital cuisine.

Simon
After the pizza, we were allowed to stay in the birthing

room for another couple of hours, but eventually we had to move to a regular hospital ward (ugh!) where at least I was able to stay and spend the night with Alex and François, albeit by sleeping in a chair as opposed to sharing Alex's bed. The vast difference from the relative calm of the birthing suite (despite the violent animal shrieks from Alex during labor) and the ward was the hospital nurse who entered and wanted to take François to be circumcised. No way, we said, and yet despite our refusal we would be asked again and again before we escaped from the hospital at 10 the following morning.

Although my father was Dutch and born in a country where practically no babies are circumcised, I happened to be born in Australia in 1964 when the circumcision rate was 95 percent. Once we'd discovered that our first child was a boy, I remember asking Alex her views on this practice and stating my own before I gave her a chance to answer. I was relieved that she was also anti-circumcision and another potentially contentious issue between us was as usual a nonevent.

Alex

When I became pregnant with François, we immediately started planning for a second child and decided to try for baby number two ASAP after his birth. It took a bit longer than we expected for me to become pregnant again, but on Simon's birthday in 2005 we were thrilled to see a double line once again. After a quick calculation, we realized that the age difference would be almost exactly two years. We called the midwife who attended François' birth, and were happy to hear that she'd started her own private practice in Brooklyn. Since we'd learned François' gender before the birth we couldn't contain our curiosity, and decided to go ahead and find out whether we'd be buying a whole new wardrobe, dressing our daughter as a tomboy or passing down brand new things François never wore to a new little brother. We had two names ready to go, and soon learned we were expecting Johan William, not Lola Augusta. While I would have enjoyed honoring Granny Lola and Great-Grandmother Anna Augusta Alexander, I was already eagerly anticipating two boys growing up together, fighting, plotting and sticking up for one another.

With Johan there was no morning sickness at all, though I still avoided taxis just in case. By the time he was on the way, I'd completely eliminated fast food and soda from my diet, and got plenty of exercise lugging 18-month-old François up and down the stairs of our co-op building, where our triplex apartment started on the fourth floor. Before he was born we bought the townhouse we live in now, and my workout routine consisted of going up and down the stoop, and carrying François any time he asked. I remember one day he had a meltdown about sitting in the stroller, and I put him on my shoulders. People looked strangely at an eight-months-pregnant woman pushing an empty stroller with an almost two-year-old on my shoulders, but I didn't care.

There were a couple of medical issues with Johan—at the beginning it seemed the placenta was dangerously close to my cervix, which could have completely ruled out vaginal delivery. As he and the uterus grew, though, it moved up and out of the way. Then there was the time we tested my blood sugar after eating cake, not exactly a smart idea. All in all, a pretty drama-free pregnancy once again. Simon's mum, Elaine, arrived from Australia to help out—my mom had come for François' birth and planned to arrive to meet Johan shortly after Elaine left so as to minimize traffic in the house and maximize time spent with the boys. As our midwives Stacey and Abby were in private practice with a smallish client list, most of Johan's prenatal appointments took place in our home, which could not have been better. The curious toddler was able to see what was going on with Mommy's belly, and didn't have to stay still in a doctor's office or examination room once he'd had a look and was bored.

We were determined not to flip out and head to the hospital too early with Johan, as that had been boring and anxiety producing the first time around. Arriving 25 minutes prior to birth, however, was cutting it a little bit fine!

By November 6, 2005 Johan was three days late and we were both getting antsy. After the due date hiccup with François, we were both worried that something similar might have happened with Johan's due date and sure enough we found ourselves at the three days overdue mark with no birth in sight. We tried walking home from Simon's office in Midtown, down Broadway and across the Brooklyn Bridge, despite the fact that we were both in business attire and shoes. Johan responded by falling asleep. The next evening our midwife, Stacey, came to the house and did some stretching and Rolfing of my ever-swelling delicate bits. By the next morning, Tuesday, November 8, I was certain the day had come, and made a tactical error by not heading to the polls and voting first thing in the morning. At least it wasn't a presidential election! I felt twinges at 11 a.m. and we gave Stacey a call after lunch, who recommended a bath and a touch base at 2 p.m. At 1:15 I somehow got myself out of the tub, got dressed and grabbed a towel for the water that broke on the way out the door. We hollered to Simon's mum that we were off, hopping in the car service rather than walking the 10 blocks as we'd planned. We arrived at the hospital at 1:50, and at 2:15 Johan flew out, landing in Stacey's capable hands. Simon was a logistical star throughout: simultaneously filling the tub, hooking up the iPod, spinning Björk and setting up the video camera. He got every moment of Johan's emergence on tape.

When we arrived at Long Island College Hospital in Brooklyn Heights, Stacey hadn't arrived yet as it was so last minute. We were shuffled through maternity triage and told I had to stay on a fetal monitor for at least 20 minutes before I could be "qualified" to be released to the birthing center. As Simon puffed up his chest and prepared for battle, we were incredibly lucky to see a familiar face. Elissa, a midwife from Elizabeth Seton, was taking on extra work as a labor and delivery nurse, and happened to be on duty. Although it had been over two years since we'd seen each other, she jumped in and ran interference for us, and after giving me a once over, disconnected the monitor and announced to the triage staff that she was taking me upstairs before I gave birth right there on the floor.

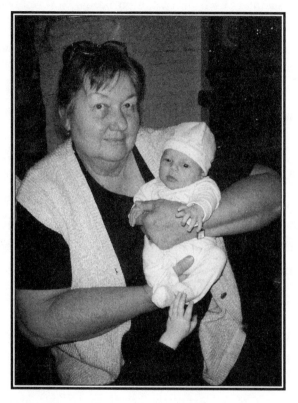

Newborn Johan with Elaine (Simon's mum)

The one thing not to love about a short labor was the aftershock. Having had such an amazing experience the first time, my expectations were pretty high for the adrenaline rush and glowing moments of bonding. Instead, I continued to have heavy contractions for several minutes afterward. Johan was fussy, too, and didn't immediately latch on to nurse as François had; we both sort of had whiplash. After about 15 minutes we both calmed down and were able to begin enjoying each other. Simon brought in Tex-Mex, a champagne split for me and a pitcher of gin and tonic in a plastic bottle for him. His mum, Elaine, arrived shortly thereafter and we all sat down to relax.

I've always been stubborn about wanting to do things my way, and was intent on proving (to myself, I guess) that I could have a newborn and a toddler and still hang on to my identity. Part of that includes not lying low—so the first thing I did as a mom of two was walk home from the hospital. We were only a few blocks away from the house, and we proudly walked home with newborn Johan in the infant seat and François riding on the buggy board behind him.

Simon
The thing I learned from one birth to the next was that I wanted to avoid having our sons scream in pain if it was unnecessary. Since the 1960s all babies born in the U.S.A. are tested for phenylketonuria (PKU), a genetic illness that can lead to mental disabilities, and in New York State this test must be given in the hospital prior to discharge, irrespective of what time the parents and baby leave. No one bothered to point out that if we left the hospital before 24 hours passed, the test results wouldn't count. We learned this the hard way much to François' pain and were determined not to repeat our mistake with Johan. François was born in the early evening and by noon

the following day we were hurtling across the Brooklyn Bridge in a Yellow Taxi on our way to our then home, Park Slope. Prior to leaving the hospital François was taken to have his heel pricked so blood could be drawn for the PKU test, but as this was conducted within 24 hours of birth we were told we'd have to have him tested again. This we did at our pediatrician's and in fact it took a total of three tests—three goes by different nurses squeezing his heel for enough blood to fill the blotter paper before a valid test was performed. So when Johan came along at 2:15 p.m. we knew we'd not only stay the night, but this time we'd stay in the hospital so that at 2:16 the following day he could have just one PKU test and not rack up his older brother's record of three.

---

10 THINGS WE'LL REMEMBER THAT HAPPENED DURING PREGNANCIES:

10. Threw up while crossing Eighth Avenue, before I was showing. People around me thought I was hungover.

9. At the airport in St. Martin, Simon whispered that a guy was checking me out from behind. I turned around to face him and he was shocked to see my belly. "I didn't know you were pregnant," he exclaimed.

---

8.   A rolling pin is great for massaging your lower back during contractions.

7.   Walking up 14 flights of stairs in August 2003 during the big citywide blackout. Although I was seven months pregnant, I wanted to go to the roof of the hotel to see something I'd never seen in the middle of a big city before: a sky full of stars. It was spectacular and worth the climb.

6.   Don't let anyone tell you what to do. Women have been having babies for thousands of years.

5.   Diane von Furstenberg wrap dresses are a practically perfect design for pregnant women.

4.   In order to keep François occupied during prenatal appointments, we got him involved by letting him help take my blood pressure, etc.

3.   Best advice I heard: men's genitals grow and change shape regularly, then go back to the way they were before. Don't worry about your female delicate bits being able to retract.

2. Pregnant women are neither aliens nor invalids. However, far be it from me to suggest that women should not use that incorrect assumption to their advantage when trying to get a seat on a crowded subway train.

1. Number one thing to bring to your hospital birth: a third-party advocate during labor who is willing to burn down the hospital to get your needs met—someone who isn't the medical provider and who isn't you. Some people hire a doula—for me that was Simon.

Chapter 2

No Sleep 'Til Brooklyn, What's My Name Again? and Who is This Alien?

The First Six Months

Simon

One of the great advantages I found by having my first child reasonably later in life (I was 39 when François was born) was that my career was relatively secure. As the general manager of a well-run hotel operation, I could largely drop out and stay home. And so with the support of the owner and my great staff behind me, I did just that for the first two weeks of his life. The only hiccup to this was my executive assistant had just resigned and in the midst of the birth I hired a new assistant fairly blindly who, while I was being thrown in at the deep end of fatherhood, was being thrown in the deep end to manage my office as I worked from home. At this time PDAs with e-mail capability were still not in common use, but I was never more than a phone call away. After we brought François home, not only did we have to get used to a new being in our existence, but our two cats also had to as well.

Alex

When François was 16 days old, we were in London midway through our first trip away from home since the birth. We were both determined to get out of town and travel as soon after the birth as possible, partly as a getaway and partly just to prove to ourselves that becoming parents didn't mean staying at home all the time. I'd read so much advice for new moms that to me seemed condescending and presumptive, such as, "You won't want to do anything for a few weeks, you won't feel like going anywhere" and my reaction was, "Well, that's NOT ME." I didn't plan to climb Mount Kilimanjaro or anything too crazy, but a trip to London? Easy! I wanted to prove to myself that I was still me and that Simon and I could simultaneously be good first-time parents obsessed with our new baby, and normal city dwellers who did normal things, like go out for late meals and travel. We continued to do so, just with a peacefully sleeping baby tucked into his stroller or car seat.

The only thing on our London agenda that didn't involve the baby was a two-hour cocktail party for the luxury hotel conference Simon attended. The party was two blocks from the hotel and we organized a sitter in the form of Simon's best man, Eddie, from our wedding, who also happened to be the director of finance of the hotel we stayed in. He came upstairs directly after work and played with, or rather walked the floor with, spaced-out François, who was wide awake and looking as far as his two-week-old eyes could see at the new person holding him and whispering to him all sorts of inside information with which to tease his father later on. It was the first time I put on a cocktail dress post-partum, and played it safe with a blazer on top. I had had my hair done in the hotel earlier while François nursed under the cape, and couldn't quite believe that I was two blocks away from my newborn, wearing makeup and a pre-pregnancy dress, standing and conversing with people. That evening everyone had seen us in New York a month earlier at a sales road show for the hotel Simon managed, and couldn't believe how "sprightly and well rested" I seemed. "Let me tell you," I said, "it's all smoke and mirrors. I'm about to collapse and slide under the piano and a drink is not even necessary." It was so surreal—someone also joked that I mustn't have even had a baby, that it was all a ruse with a fake belly and we were laughing at them all. It was all too real when we scurried back to our room and found our new baby who was just becoming hungry and looking around for his mom. I quickly changed, snuggled up into an armchair and fell asleep with François attached to me while the guys ordered a bottle of wine and Simon made Ed give him an exact play-by-play of every move they made in the two hours.

Life with a new baby is exciting and exhausting, as anyone who has been through it will tell you. In hindsight it seems harder than it did to me at the time, because there was such a constant adrenaline rush and everything was such a new experience. Nevertheless, there were times when Simon went to work and I was at home with the baby, looking around at the laundry to be done, the newspapers thrown everywhere, the sink full of dishes to be dealt with and hungry cats yowling for a refill of bowls, which I couldn't bend down far enough to reach because François was sleeping in the carrier on my chest. One day I took a photo of the Greek tragedy our dining room had become, just for posterity. Taking that photo was helpful for my sanity and proved that these messes that happened in the space of three minutes were truly real and not exaggerated. The break that I got to find the camera, take the picture, download it and e-mail it to Simon allowed me to regroup enough to face cleaning it up 15 minutes later, and not put the baby in a FedEx box to send to my mother. When François was born we didn't have a housekeeper or a regular babysitter, nor did we have any family in the city. It could have been isolating and depressing, but I forced myself out the door most days, even if for nothing more than a walk through the autumn leaves covering the city.

We were very, very lucky that after getting over their initial shock at entering the world we had two good sleepers. Once we moved them out of our bed and into their own, we had a few cry-it-out nights with François and virtually none with Johan. We felt well equipped to bring a baby into our bed and never had a problem rolling onto either of them. Certainly some do argue against co-sleeping, but Simon and I both slept with cats and dogs our whole lives without squishing them, and neither of us drank to excess or took sleeping pills. I became pretty adept at nursing on my side while (sort of) sleeping, which delayed the problem of leaping out of bed at regular intervals. One concession we made was to keep an infant car seat right next to the bed, and used it a few times. That also made us more comfortable when we had been out to dinner late and they fell asleep at the restaurant—we just brought the car seat out of the cab and straight into our room with no wake-ups. Another sneaky thing I did to get more sleep was put François in a king bed with bumpers on either side of him. This worked well for the first two months out of our bed, then once he began to roll we put him in a portable crib. While he was in the king bed, I could crawl in next to him to nurse if he woke up, and by the time we moved him into the Pack n' Play at four or five months he was sleeping through the night most of the time. As a result, we never bought an actual crib for the boys. They went from our bed to a big bed to a Pack n' Play to a twin bed between 18 months and two years, pretty much without incident. Johan spent a few nights in the Bugaboo bassinet because he liked it for some reason. We didn't avoid the big wooden crib for any reason other than convenience, and it worked well for us.

Simon

I have to say looking back now over six years later, the rose-colored glasses of which Alex wrote are firmly in place and for the life of me I find it hard to recall too many negatives. The wonderment of seeing black tar emanate from your new baby was hardly a negative. Nor even was the midnight race to the 24-hour pharmacy to buy a breast pump as Alex's breasts were seemingly engorged with too much milk and she thought they were about to explode and fly off her chest. Frankly the hardest thing was probably the few times I held a crying Alex some four months or more after François was born. She was upset because he was then sleeping in another room and screaming for her, not out of hunger but merely missing her skin and not really liking his newfound nocturnal solitude. Before too long he learned to sleep throughout the night and to this day both he and Johan, with whom we also adopted the "cruel to be kind" sleeping strategy, have blessed us with mostly disturbance-free nights ever since. Thanks, guys.

Alex
Lest one think the first six months were perfect, let me tell you—they weren't. I had terrible trouble pumping milk with François, and ended up taking him everywhere. Or (when we absolutely had to get a sitter) I'd leave formula as backup while we were out and then pump as soon as we got home to relieve the pressure and to build up a store of frozen milk. I never wanted formula to touch their lips, but it did on occasion, though I'm happy to say they both nursed on demand until they weaned themselves. François abruptly quit nursing at just under a year, and Johan held steady until about 16 months.

Another problem we encountered was Simon's frustration with my mommy-brain, and my frustration with both his frustration and myself. Sometimes it seems as though the lack of sleep and general order to new moms' lives causes a loss of IQ points, but I've always been of the "never let them see you sweat" mentality, and did my best to appear put together at all times. I did this pretty well during the first six months of each boy's life, so well sometimes that I even fooled my husband, who then resumed thinking of me as a normal person capable of a decent day's output and on occasion wondered why the laundry wasn't done, dinner wasn't on the table and I wasn't out looking for more acting or design work when he got home, when all I really wanted to do was lay down and die from exhaustion. This expectation worked both ways: I have always been an overachiever and relentlessly whipped myself to see how much I could accomplish for the baby, myself and the household each day.

I was so obsessive about it that I felt as though I needed to go to confession if I even turned on the television or picked up a book during the day. I remember I so desperately wanted to a) feel like a normal person and b) be useful and productive that I went a little crazy. Simon began to appear to me as an alien from the land of effectiveness—someone who could actually wake up at a normal time, shower and put on a suit, go to his office and be useful all day. I was jealous of his routine and normality, and wondered whether I'd ever feel like that again. It didn't help that my two professions were either freelance or, well, ephemeral would be putting it charitably. Prior to François' birth I was fighting in the trenches of acting, trying to find a breakout role. I was beginning to build some momentum around the time

I became pregnant and it was heartbreaking to be written off once I started to show, although when pregnant with Johan I was fortunate to do a movie with people who made a character pregnant for me. To then go out and fight for parts or design contracts when I was so loopy and out of it (for example, staring blankly at my computer screen and not being able to remember my full name) was difficult. I hoped that being in an altered state would spur my creativity with graphic design, but really all I could do was hold on to the one client I had at the time instead of finding new ones. After François was a year old I did manage to get some fresh on-site freelance work, and it was beyond weird to go into an office where no one knew me and or that I had a baby.

Simon

With Johan's birth approaching, Alex and I were both concerned with how our two-year-old would react to a newcomer who'd be challenging him for our attention. We discussed this and decided that I'd take the lead with François and let her concentrate on Johan. At that point, François was a rambunctious toddler who loved to play with Daddy, and I was a daddy who loved to play with him. While this delegation of children made sense at the time, it also led to a quandary in that Alex and I separately were worried that with my concentration on François I was missing out on bonding and developing a relationship with Johan and him with me. In fact, I had to make a conscious effort to spend less time with François and more with Johan, which with me away from the house working nine plus hours a day wasn't that easy. As our first year being parents to two children went on, François developed a regular sleep pattern of 11 hours a night while Johan napped throughout the day and slept for about seven hours at night. Eventually we all slipped into a nice pattern that worked where Alex would put François to bed at 7:30 p.m. or so and I would spend a good hour alone with Johan until she returned, gave him a final feed for the night and then he went to bed as well.

I have to admit that it probably took a full year for my feelings for Johan to rival those of François and whether or not that's typical of how fathers react to second and subsequent children, that's how it was for me. Now, they are well into their second and fourth years of school at the ripe old ages of four and six, and I can honestly say that there is no difference with the intensity of my love for each of them. In hindsight it's hard to believe there was ever a stage when there was.

One of the challenges I expected to face as a father, and perhaps I'm not there yet, is that I have no immediate role model from my own life to emulate (or to not emulate as the case may be). Two months before my sixth birthday my father died and my mother, at the young age of 32, was suddenly the sole parent to four children whose ages were 13 months, almost six, nine and 11 years old. She didn't remarry until 18 years later and so throughout my entire childhood and the remainder of the time I spent living in Australia my parenting was solely conducted by a woman.

Sure, I watched Fred McMurray in *My Three Sons* as a young boy, but I'm not sure that those secondhand childhood memories of a fictional TV program featuring fatherhood in America were going to help me much when it came time to be a dad myself.

Simon, His Father (François) and Baby Brother Adam

I suppose the abiding promise I made to myself and Alex (and silently to the boys) was that I was determined to last on this planet long after their sixth birthdays... and 16th and 26th and perhaps even Johan's 36th as well. Here's hoping.

TOP 10 MEMORIES OF RANDOM THINGS WE DID WHILE IN THE POST-BIRTH HAZE:

10. While changing François' diaper on day one or two, we both stood mesmerized by the changing pad as meconium oozed out of him. It was really the most bizarre and fascinating thing I'd seen to date.

9. We took baby Johan for drinks at the Mercer Kitchen when he was 48 hours old.

8. Alex – I worked as a location manager on a low-budget film produced by childless 20-somethings, buzzing around Manhattan and Brooklyn negotiating space deals with François strapped to my chest. This was the first nakedly anti-baby prejudice I experienced, and the only time in my life so far I ever resigned from a job.

7. Alex – I literally cried with gratitude when Simon gave me an espresso machine for my first birthday as a mom.

6. We subversively took sleeping babies to as many non-child-friendly places as possible to prove the point that children can be seen, not heard and not bothersome,

such as dinner at the Ritz in London, the Sahara Desert, shopping on Madison Avenue, Underbar in Union Square and film festivals.

5. Simon – I took three-month-old François to see kangaroos in a paddock near my mother's house when we visited, and let him grab their fur and even "ride" one. Of course in photos it looks like I was trying to feed him to them.

Baby François = Wallaby Food?

4. Alex – Screamed at my husband while he held me in a quasi-headlock to prevent me

from going into François' room for yet a fourth time in the middle of the night after we'd both agreed to let him cry it out.

3. Simon – When Johan was born, introducing François to his baby brother in the hospital. He very carefully held Johan on Alex's lap and whispered, "Hi, Johan. Hi, baby." The wonder in his two-year-old voice was clear.

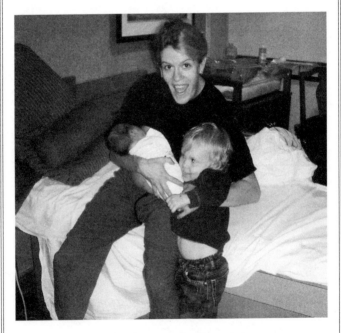

Hi, Baby! François Meets Johan

2. We took one-week-old François out in the Baby Björn to see the New York Marathon, as the route was one block from our apartment at the time. It took us a moment to realize why no one was standing on the opposite side of the road, where we'd gone for a better view. Of course, once the runners started to clog the road, we wouldn't get back across for an hour, so we literally sprinted across the street with the baby just in time.

1. Alex – Did not even try to squeeze myself into pre-maternity trousers for about a month—I continued to wear maternity jeans with draped sweaters, and gradually eased myself back into pre-baby clothes.

Chapter 3

The Screaming Kid on the Plane is NOT Mine! (This Time)

Traveling with Children

Alex

> **Hotel Bartender Marrakech (HB):** Ce n'est pas pos-
> sible se d'asseoir avec votre bébé dans la bar.
>
> **Moi:** Pourquoi?
>
> **HB:** Parce que les gens fument.
>
> **Moi:** Mais maintenant il n'y personne a fumer.
>
> **HB:** Mais peut'etre c'est possible.
>
> **Moi:** J'attends mon mari et mes amis, juste 10 minutes
> peut'etre. Si quelqu'un entre et commence à fumer, je
> prendrai le bébé à l'extérieur.

(The bartender, convinced that in the 10 minutes I waited for
Simon and our friends in the hotel bar someone might come
in and blow smoke in five-week-old François' face, looked at
me disapprovingly for the entire 10 minutes. Meanwhile, I

enjoyed my glass of champagne and François slept on, never knowing that he was in the bar to begin with.)

Alex, Baby François and a Camel Drive

We've traveled in every class of service since we've been parents, and on pretty much every type of aircraft imaginable, from the six-seater to the largest Boeings and Airbuses. Along the way there have been boats, trains, cars, limos and even a pickup truck or two. Both sides of my family are from Texas, and I grew up traveling between Dallas, Fort Scott (a small town in Kansas where I went to school) and the Caribbean where my family had a house. We've taken the boys to Africa, Australia, all over Europe and the States and many, many islands. We've obsessively taken pictures of sleeping babies in front of Big Ben, the Sydney Opera

House, the St. Tropez Harbor and the Atlas Mountains as proof they were there, because of course they won't remember the early trips. Our boys have been licked by kangaroos, sniffed by camels, placed sleeping in their car seats under tables during long dinners in France and have played in more than one airplane closet. Once the seat belt sign was off, of course. Maybe.

The thing that really gets me is hearing parents complain about how hard it is to travel with young children. Guess what? They are right; it IS hard. It can be a complete pain in the you-know-what in fact. We get that, but we've never let that stop us from going! I was on a commercial flight recently by myself, and the grass is not always greener. When you fly by yourself, there's no one to watch your carry-on while you go to the bar. What, you don't go to the bar? Oh, dear. OK, here's another one—when going through security, you have to deal with everything yourself, and there's no one to talk to when the inevitable delays occur. Besides, with whom are you going to laugh at the wildly entertaining things you see in the airport, like the completely drunk guy being hauled off by security in one of those little golf carts? At 3:30 in the afternoon. You had to wonder where they were going—the chapel, perhaps? Unless you are driven by limo to a private hangar where your Gulfstream jet is waiting to whisk you away, the act of getting from one part of the world to another has become a lot harder than it was when we were kids. Remember when we didn't need ID to get on a domestic flight, it was OK to sleep on the floor as long as you didn't block the aisle and you could congregate near the bathrooms and galleys? These days it's a very lucky day if our boys get a chance to peek inside the cockpit and wave to the pilots, as opposed to an early memory I have of being allowed to plunk myself down in the copilot's chair and touch things. That may have been against the rules even in the '70s, but it was a different time. Point being, with all the security measures designed to ~~annoy us~~ keep us safe, these days the journey is less relaxing than it has ever been. Simon and I have made the decision to keep traveling with the kids, and focus on the destination.

François Touring Sydney by Osmosis

Australia

Last year we went to visit Simon's family in Australia, and it was the first time we'd made the trip with both boys. As he is one of four siblings, all of whom get around the globe to varying degrees, they all take turns visiting one another. The last time we'd headed down under was when François was three months old and we'd proudly flown first class on British Airways with our brand-new baby. He slept most of the way and charmed flight attendants when he was awake, one of whom said how much better behaved he was than the infant of an Oscar-winning actress who had been on the same flight the week before. Apparently that one had been a colicky screamer who kept the whole cabin from sleeping.

Fast forward five years and we were off to Oz again, this time on a direct New York/Los Angeles/Sydney run rather than a leisurely round-the-world trip due to work commitments at home. Having just invested quite a lot of money in remodeling our house, the five-figure price tag on four first-class or business-class seats felt like a ridiculous extravagance, and we hadn't planned far enough in advance to secure seats on miles. We booked ourselves in coach and prepared for the worst. For the first leg, we were due to leave JFK at 6:30 p.m. and land in L.A. at the east coast equivalent of 1:30 a.m. We decided that we'd try to keep the boys awake the whole leg so that they'd pass out on the L.A./Sydney flight. For a week leading up to the departure we put them to bed a little bit later every night, so that the night before we left, they went to bed at midnight and slept until 10:30 a.m. That actually worked really, really well.

We also packed each boy a backpack with a DVD player and a few new discs, books, stickers and little 99-cent store toys they'd never seen before and were expendable if lost or broken. We sat in two rows, one adult per child, and it was really great to have forced time to focus on just one boy, have a real conversation and spend time together with no interruptions from the other child or parent.

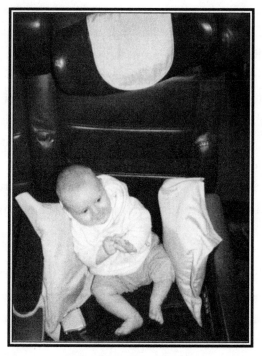

First-Class François

Simon

As this trip was after we'd become known to the public and our boys' behavior or rather unruly behavior had become internet gossip fodder, I wondered whether people would notice them on the flight and watch them hoping for antics. Sure enough, a discussion topic on a parenting website surfaced the day after we arrived in Australia—the husband of one of the moms who frequented this blog was on our flight. He dutifully e-mailed his wife, who was most disappointed that the only thing to report after flying halfway around the world with us was that I made a comment to François about his bag carrying the logo of a recently defunct investment bank, and that Alex's jeans apparently had a shiny credit card-like thing on her rump. Other moms on the site were desperate for news of our rowdy boys on this 24-hour flight, but alas, as they'd neither been rude nor unruly, her husband said that there was nothing to report. However, his wife did write as a way of an excuse, that her husband took drugs to knock himself out so he would have missed their bad behavior anyway. We can happily report that her drugged-up husband missed no antics—well, from our boys anyway.

Alex

On the way back home, we sat behind a family that bought two seats for three kids. I'm all for saving money where you can, but let me put on my how-to hat for just a second and say unless it tips the scale between going on the trip versus staying home, DON'T DO THAT. After our kids were about nine to 12 months old, we always bought them a seat. I would rather get seats for everyone in a cheaper class of service than share a first- or business-class seat with any child big enough to wiggle. Anyway, on the flight from Sydney back to Los

Angeles, two of the kids in the family ahead of us were really acting up. The 18-month-old was systematically torturing his parents into insanity, and just when he fell asleep, his sister stood up over her mother on the seat and started banging on the headrest, shouting something that really sounded like, "Die! Die!" It may have been "Cry" or "Hi" or "Pie," but at that point I'd been awake for so many hours all I could do was cross my fingers that no one would think those temporarily demonic children belonged to us.

Of course in between the flights to and from Australia, we did spend two weeks on the ground there. It was the first trip for Johan and the first trip François was old enough to remember, and we had a wonderful time with family. One thing I hadn't counted on was a reminder that television can in fact be educational for kids. When we looked out our hotel window in Sydney, both boys immediately recognized the Sydney Opera House and Harbour. François had seen photos of himself there as a baby, but how did Johan know? From watching *The Wiggles*. Far be it from me to advocate TV for kids, but moderation is everything and both Simon and I were tickled to see that the kids knew exactly where they were. They had a little trouble grasping that we couldn't take a taxi from there to Coober Pedy, but nevermind, at least they knew what it was. That François learned from *Priscilla, Queen of the Desert*, an educational film in oh-so-many ways.

Long trips with young children require quite a lot of planning, but when I think back to our early trips with babies, it was really all about knowing how much or little to pack. Comparatively, traveling with an infant was easy. We took François overseas when he was less than two weeks old, and the only drama was making sure we got his passport issued in time. Knowing that in New York City it was unlikely we'd have the official birth certificate by then, we got a letter issued at the hospital confirming the birth, allowing us to get a temporary passport, which was good for a year. It was only after they were out of babyhood and able to walk and talk that flying became a little more complicated. This also coincided with the ever-strengthening security measures each time another terrorist attack was thwarted—and once the boys had tapered off nursing I remembered madly pouring milk and juice into bottles, as it was the only way the liquid would be allowed on board. I drove myself crazy with two backpacks full of drinks and snacks, when in the end taking much less would have been fine. I've always silently laughed at people who overpack, but the first few trips away with both boys I completely fell into that trap. After a couple of toddler flights I realized that it's better to just take what you need for the few hours you're on the plane, and leave the rest. Either kids will be willing to play with plastic cups, read the exit safety sheet and watch movies, or they will get antsy and scream. Regardless, the flight will eventually be over.

In fact, out of the many early trips we took, we spent more time managing our caregiver than the kids. For the first three years of Johan's life we had au pairs, and coordinating who had to take the kids to the bathroom, whose turn it was to sleep and how much time the au pair had to sightsee was the biggest job of all.

In St. Barths

Will They Remember?
In a word, no. At least not the earliest trips.

Alex: Johan, what countries have you been
           to?
Johan: Ummm, Dallas and the Hamptons.

(Both of which we'd been to in the two weeks prior
to me asking him.)

Alex :   Have you been to France?
Johan: What's France, Mama?

49

Half an hour later, we thought we'd try François.

Simon:	What's the first trip you remember, F-Boy?
François:	Africa.
Alex:	Wow, you remember that trip?
François:	I just know that I went.
Simon:	How do you know?
François:	Because you told me!

Our six-year-old does not actually remember being in Australia at the age of three months, nor does he remember being in Monte Carlo or Italy at the age of three years. He does, however, understand that he was there with us when we talk about the trips, and recognizes himself in photos of all the places we've been together. When he went back to Oz at the age of five, he knew that he'd been there before and was excited to see all the things "he missed" the first time, like petting the kangaroos as opposed to being held by Daddy in a photo next to one. He recognizes the big carousels one sees everywhere in France as being French, and will always ask if photos of him or Johan riding one were taken in France—he was only wrong once, and it was Monaco so close enough! A fun addition to the experience is when we go somewhere we'd been previously with François only, and return with Johan. François becomes the big brother travel guide, regardless of whether he remembers anything about the place. Now whenever we travel, Johan asks, "Have I been there before?" Both boys know that we like to travel and to take them with us, which makes them feel special. They are excited to see new places and have new experiences, and pick up on the fact that Simon and I are excited, too—we share in the fun. That is the best takeaway from gallivanting across the galaxy with minors. We have two relatively fearless kids who love seeing new things and are excited to share adventures with Mom and Dad.

ALEX'S TOP 10 TRAVEL MEMORIES:

10. A late dinner in Cannes, with one-month-old Johan asleep in his car seat under the table.

9. The complete change in mood when two bored boys on a car trip in Australia suddenly saw a kangaroo in a paddock.

8. A great photo of François riding a reindeer with fake snow on the beach in the south of France.

7. Sitting in a gorgeous orchard in Morocco while nursing François.

6. Walking with baby Johan in a sling in Italy, marveling that after nearly 10 years I still

---

remembered enough Italian to brag about my baby to an interested stranger.

5. Being silently offered multiple glasses of wine by a sympathetic flight attendant during a flight from hell back from overseas with two cranky boys, a passed-out-from-exhaustion husband and an au pair with the flu.

4. François gleefully peeling off layer upon layer of bunting once he came inside during a winter weekend in Montreal.

3. Johan watching in amazement as a large turtle devoured the hibiscus flower he'd offered it.

Two Boys and a Hungry Turtle

2. Both boys charging down Saline Beach in St. Barths like something out of *Lord of the Flies.*

1. Seeing the look of recognition on three-year-old François' face after we drove from France into Italy and he realized the language changed.

Chapter 4

"Mommy, Johan is Gone!"

When Accidents Happen

Nothing can prepare you for the feeling of absolute help-lessness when your child gets hurt, and you get to the point where you realize that there is nothing more you can do to help them. This hit home when a recent accident happened.

Alex
We were meant to be in Atlantic City for 24 hours—a limo ride down from New York Saturday morning, the afternoon spent playing on the boardwalk with the boys, a panel dis-cussion that evening, breakfast and more boardwalk playing en famille Sunday morning and a ride back home. Somehow our worst family accidents seem to happen outside of New York—maybe we should never leave! We arrived on Saturday as planned and met up with friends at a neighboring hotel. The boys immediately joined forces with two sisters of simi-lar ages and proceeded to have a grand old time splashing

each other in the pool. We lounged in a cabana near the edge of the pool and caught up with the other adults, had a fruit platter and generally acknowledged that in that moment, life was good. Simon walked to the edge of the pool and began chatting with François, when *it* happened. The metal plate covering the bolts on the railing to the stairs was loose, and François' big toe got caught underneath when he waded up the stairs to get out of the pool. His toe had been cut. At that point all we knew was that the cut was very deep, blood was everywhere and François was in shock.

Security navigated us through the crowd and down to the entrance to a waiting cab to the nearest ER, which luckily on a Saturday afternoon was empty. We received the news that François' tendon had been severed, which hit us hard, and we began to think of our options. He would need orthopedic surgery to repair the tendon. As the cut happened just after lunch, the earliest the procedure could begin was 9 p.m. due to the necessity of an eight-hour fasting period before undergoing anesthesia. In order to avoid him having to spend the night in the hospital, we decided to have the wound closed temporarily and foot immobilized and we scheduled the surgery for early the next morning.

Since François wouldn't be able to eat for eight hours, we tried to minimize his discomfort by giving him a huge dinner and waking him up right before it was time to go back to the hospital. He was not in pain, and the shock had worn off to the point that he would have bounded around the hotel room that night in his splint if we'd allowed it. We explained to him that he needed to have a doctor fix the tendon, that he would have to go to sleep while it happened and he would be given medicine to make him go to sleep. Of course the hardest part for François was not eating. By the time he was ready to be taken to the operating theatre at about 10:30 a.m., he had been awake for two and a half hours, and had never before waited that long to have any food or drink, although they had him on a fluid IV. He looked at me forlornly and said, "I know I'm not supposed to have anything, but Mommy, I'm so hungry." I hugged him and tried not to completely break down; I still can't get over how brave he was.

While François was in the operating room, we coped in different ways. Simon took multiple walks to Starbucks and got on the phone, funneling information to relatives and friends who knew about the incident. I stayed with Johan, who was clearly aware of what had happened, but still a pretty normal three-year-old. I played with him and tried to keep calm. Knowing the risks of general anesthesia, I was terrified that some kind of complication would happen. I thought of him going into cardiac arrest on the table, or of a piece of gauze being left in the wound and becoming infected. I thought of scar tissue building up and interfering with François' ability to walk normally. My mind went a little crazy and I even thought of having to make phone calls to tell people that we'd lost him. I remembered being five years old myself, and holding my father's hand as he cried when he got the news that his son, my half-brother, had been killed in a car accident driving home from college. I then snapped back to reality and played with Johan, and my mind went off on another tangent. I thought of the kids and teens I knew growing up who had suffered debilitating accidents or had died. In the years we've been parents, François has been the most accident-prone, and the only one who had ever been to the ER or needed stitches. Did that mean that when Johan grew up to be a teenager, he'd be killed in a car accident or hit by a bus while riding his bicycle? Was Johan saving up all his nine lives to go out with a bang later on? Would either of them, or the two little girls who had been in the pool at the time of the accident, have nightmares about all the blood? As it turned out, I needn't have worried about the girls. They got out of the pool and told their mother, "He got hurt, but his parents are there." The fact of the matter is that once you make the commitment to having children, there's always the possibility that something terrible could happen to them, just as one of us or our loved ones could get killed on the road. Although the statistics were in our favor, bad things do happen. I kept trying to bring myself to focus on getting through the hour, and spoke politely to a few *Housewives* fans who approached and wondered what had happened. This was an additional wrinkle—it was the first time any one of us had needed medical treatment since we became more recognizable than the average family, and everyone at the hospital seemed to know we were there. One young woman who was a hospital employee participating in a disaster drill came up to us covered in latex wounds, and I was so out of it that for a moment I thought she was actually injured. She said she regretted seeing us there because it meant someone was hurt, and that she hoped everything turned out well.

Simon

One of the most magical experiences of parenting is watching young babies, toddlers and children before they're affected by the norms of social behavior. Fear is seemingly a learned behavior as we scream and run to stop the crawling baby going near the top of the stairs lest it pivot and tumble down. Fear might be based on the unknown, à la the bogeyman looming in the dark, but simultaneously one can argue that sometimes ignorance is bliss and protects one from experiencing fear. François knew not what to expect as he went off to the operating theatre other than he was going to have a little sleep and while he was so doing his toe would be fixed. So while his parents were madly cramping inside with the knowledge of the risks of general anesthesia on young children, we were delightfully brought back to reality and the here and now by his younger brother, Johan. While not showing any lack of concern for his big brother, Johan continually reassured us that François would be fine and they'd soon be happily splashing each other in the pool again. This trip was François' fifth visit to the ER and fortunately his first (and hopefully) last involving major surgery. For the 90 minutes he was in surgery and the first few in recovery before we all joined him to watch him wake up, Johan kept Alex and me sane. Honestly, if it had just been us, those 90 minutes would have been far harder and longer. Johan, thanks!

By the way, at the time of writing the ER score is François 5, Johan 0!

Alex

Sometimes the incident isn't an injury, but it's no less trau-
matic. One afternoon two years ago I was in the kitchen
prepping Chicken Tikka Masala, a family favorite. For
years this was a must-order dish on our takeout menu, but
after our first gut-renovation in 2002, I decided to learn
how to make it. It's not that difficult, and I realized when
going through our year-end expenses that we'd spent nearly
$5,000 on Indian takeout. Not a good use of money when
we both cook! At the time our kitchen was on the ground
floor and had two large windows facing into the garden
where the boys were outside playing together. I had an eye
on them mostly, but was also concentrating on measuring
spices and marinating chicken. Suddenly, François came
running in the garden door shouting, "Mommy, Johan's
gone!" It's not a cliché to say that a lump rose into my throat
and I had to catch my breath as I felt sick to my stomach.
"I think he evaporated," François said. I ran outside and
surveyed the backyard. It's not a large area (about 22 feet
by 40 feet), it's completely fenced in and there are only so
many places a one and a half-year-old boy can hide. I called
to him; no answer. I checked under the Japanese willows at
the back fence; no Johan. I checked the kitchen again just
to be 100 percent sure he hadn't slithered past me and gone
into the house… no. I went back outside, and thought, even
though we are surrounded on all sides by high fences, is
there any possible way out of this garden? Just then I heard
a noise, which sounded very much like a frustrated toddler.
The property next door to us had recently been renovated

and there was a retaining wall blocked only by boards. Sure enough, there was a space of a few inches where the boards had settled. I shimmied through it myself, tightrope-walked across the retaining wall to find, at the end, Johan shouting in righteous indignation while trying to lower himself into the garden of the next house, two houses away from us. I grabbed him in an emotional rush, darted back across the retaining wall with him in my arms (perhaps not the smartest thing to do in heels) and carried him to safety. Shortly thereafter the boards were secured and we all moved on, but I have had aftershocks of fear when I remember François' worried little voice asking, "Mommy, where did he go?"

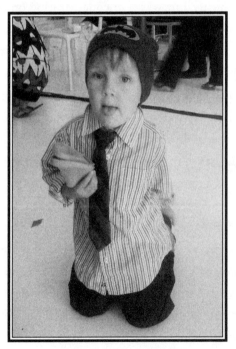

Johan Amusing Himself

Johan has proven to be a slippery little fellow. He is very independent and plays extremely well by himself, but when he's had enough, he sometimes decides to leave in search of the next adventure. In all other respects he's very careful, and never runs out into the street or copies some of the daredevil moves of his older brother, however, he's been known to simply walk away when he's bored. During filming for season one of *The Real Housewives*, we shot a scene with the midwives who delivered both our boys. We were in Prospect Park, the Brooklyn equivalent of Central Park, at a picnic with lots of other parents. There came a time when the crew wanted to get a conversation between the adults, and the kids were allowed to play with the other children attending the picnic under the eye of a production assistant. The lesson learned that day was to never let someone who isn't a parent watch children if they are also doing something else. It's a lot to ask a non-parent who doesn't normally babysit and is also on the job to continue doing their job while keeping an eye on a mobile child. After we'd filmed the 10-minute scene, we grabbed François and looked for Johan in order to pack up and move to the next location, as we had multiple set-ups to shoot that day. He was nowhere to be seen. Panic ensued, not only among us, but the crew, the midwives and the other parents. Somehow our 20-month-old had managed to evade everyone and take off. After a minute or two, we found him under a nearby tree counting leaves, completely happy and curious as to why we all seemed so upset. If François needs to be encased in bubble wrap,

Johan needs a GPS tracking device embedded into his sneakers.

We'll knock on wood that nothing bad has ever happened in a place where we don't speak the language and are completely stranded. We've been going to St. Barths, an island in the French West Indies section of the Caribbean, for six years running now, and absolutely love it for a number of reasons. One plus we hadn't thought about much is that it has become a home away from home. Take last summer for example. On the second day there, we were having lunch and checking e-mail at our favorite outdoor restaurant, now called Caviar Island (though to me it will always be Le Square) in Gustavia, the capital. The boys had finished their bird-like lunches and were playing at and around the table in the Cour Vendôme, just off the Carre d'Or. The shops surrounding the square were all closed for lunch, and most of the store managers were eating outside as well and chatting with the boys in a mixture of French, English and Franglais as they searched for buried treasure in the outdoor couch cushions. François fell and hit his chin, splitting it wide open and chipping a tooth. The elapsed time from the moment of impact to the time he was stitched up in the ER was 19 minutes, a record we couldn't have beat at home in NYC. We knew that on a Saturday afternoon in St. Barths during a music festival our best bet was the ER at the local hospital, and knew where it was and with whom to talk once we arrived. Why did we know all this? Because of François, of course! Two years earlier, we'd wound up in ER when a bizarre staph infection developed on his legs and the little man had a very large blister on his toe that had needed lancing. On the day of the exploding chin incident, François got laughing gas, three stitches and the only thing that required any sort of delay was getting through to our pediatrician in NYC to confirm, as we'd thought, that he'd already had his first tetanus shot. While Simon was in the operating room with François, I took Johan to the hospital playroom we'd discovered during our previous visit. We were back in the restaurant to finish lunch within the hour, with pretty much everyone we'd seen earlier still there to congratulate François on his newest war wound and to show him the underside of their own chins. I'm beginning to think everyone in the world except Simon has a scar under their chin. I know I do.

Sometimes there's drama even when the incident isn't hospital-worthy. I had to decide whether to lose my mind or laugh when Johan got a 24-hour bug. It was nothing as far as illnesses go, just a high-ish fever and a sleepy, lethargic kid. Johan didn't want to take the Tylenol I wanted to give him, either in chewable or syrup form. François turned into a big brother cheerleader and coaxed Johan through the process, proclaiming that the chewables tasted like lollipops, pouring the syrup and showing him the gummy vitamin he could have if he took the medicine. Success, and Johan was completely willing to take the second dose later that night. Fast-forward to the next day. François woke up dizzy and got worse as the day progressed. When I brought out the medicine, Johan reached for François' hand and said, "It's your turn!" Seems like a great case of brothers helping brothers, right? Well, no. Uh-uh. François wanted no part of that medicine, and kicked, screamed, had to be held down by me and our nanny, spat the medicine across the room and had a big, long timeout. Never mind that he'd spent the previous day gently coaxing Johan to do it, François would rather be closed up in his room for half an hour than take the same medicine. The chewables that the day before had tasted "like lollipops" were now "horrible, nasty things that taste like poo." Ah, the logic of a five-year-old. In the end, I had to threaten to tell Daddy, a card I hate playing because I don't like the good cop/bad cop routine, but it worked. During the drama, Johan cocked his head at François and asked, "Why don't you make sense?" Very good question, kid!

Simon
After becoming parents we realized that we not only worried about keeping the kids safe, but that we had a responsibility to them if something happened to us as well. When François was born we still hadn't got around to writing a will. And prior to that it really wasn't that necessary in that in New York State, a childless spouse, unless a will states otherwise, inherits the deceased spouse's estate. After his birth, and while we should have written wills, the main thing we did was to ask my younger brother, Adam, and his wife, Vanessa, to adopt François in the event of our simultaneous death, which was amended to include Johan after he came along. Adam and Vanessa have a son, Ties,

who is just 16 days older than François. Also to that end, when we took François to Australia at three months old, I took Alex on a tour of the school I'd attended in Brisbane, Queensland with a view to let her see the fantastic academic record and facilities and to enroll François for entry in 2016. Private school registration in Australia is very different than in NYC in that it is basically necessary to enroll your children at birth to guarantee entry, and we registered the names of first François, then Johan once he came along, in case we both died and they went to live in Australia.

Alex
It's funny how giving life can make you think of death. Prior to becoming a parent I never gave it the slightest thought, beyond a random daydream of what my funeral might look like, complete with lots of big black hats and chanting.

It took a weekend trip to Israel for a Bar Mitzvah (where the boys weren't coming) for us to finally work out our wills and contingency plans for exactly what would happen should either or both of us die (i.e., a plane crash or car accident involving both of us coming home to the boys, etc.). As we have no family in New York, it was particularly important to us to specify exactly whom should be notified if the worst happened, down to specifics such as who stays with the children while family flies in. We've only left the boys in New York twice, but thought it down to the last detail, such as airlines calling our nanny, our nanny calling my mother, etc. None of this is fun to think about, but having it done and copies sent to our executors made us breathe a bit easier. It only took us three years after having kids. Ahem.

Simon

The great strides in medical science in the last 100 plus years have meant that an awful lot of illnesses never happen, and so vaccinations, while not preventing accidents (this chapter's sub-heading), do prevent illness and worse. However the advent of the Internet has added to the information about vaccinations and for every site out there stating how important these preventative measures are, there will always be another stating that having a vaccination for disease A may, or worse, will cause condition B.

Which brings me to the dreaded swine flu, or correctly named H1N1, strain that arrived in early 2009 followed by a huge media frenzy that only succeeded in whipping up unnecessary panic. In April 2009, when the disease first struck NYC, the panic was palpable. My mum called us from Australia (which at that stage was H1N1-free) wanting to know what emergency precautions we were taking. When I said none, other than normal good hygiene practices, she sounded a little scared. Summer came and the panic subsided, but warnings came that when winter approached H1N1 would be a real threat.

Six months later with both boys in school, we received a letter home from their school stating that all children were eligible to receive the H1N1 vaccination at school providing we authorized it. Neither Alex nor I were keen for them to have it, but I found myself scared that if we stopped them from having the vaccination that we'd never forgive ourselves if they did develop the flu. There seemed little recorded negative harm from getting the vaccination, but still we debated them getting it though eventually gave the authorization. When winter came, the hysteria died away. Many people have gotten the swine flu and not died or at least if they have died, the media isn't screaming it from the rooftops like they once were.

We will probably never know whether they would have been better off being exposed to the virus and building their own antibodies or having the vaccination. Honestly deciding something like this is very much a "damned if you do, damned if you don't" situation. But as long as you've thought long and hard about the decision, then no one can fault you for deciding either way.

TOP 10 THINGS WE DO IN A CRISIS:

10. Become a superhero and put a force field around anyone under four feet tall. Seriously, we can't insulate our kids forever. They will fall, get punched by a bully or spike a ridiculous fever someday. We remind ourselves of this often.

9. Surf the web for advances in technology— as soon as they make shoes with a tracking

system in them, I'm buying 10 pairs!

8. Eventually (other parents, please be faster than us!) we got all our contingency plans in order.

7. Know what calms the kids down, such as making silly faces or reciting Shel Silverstein poetry backwards.

6. We concentrate. Even if five minutes beforehand we'd been having a petty argument about what to order for lunch, if an accident happens everyone has to drop what they are doing and help solve the problem.

5. We trust our kids. They are often rambunctious, but 99.9 percent of the time when there's a crisis, they see our focus and snap into line.

4. Since we have two kids, we get one to help us with the other. If we suddenly can't see Johan, the first person we ask is François. With two kids we have built-in witnesses.

3. We breathe. We're no good to the boys if we've passed out. If there are two parents present, at least one needs to remain calm.

2. We listen to each other. If we don't, we get in each other's way and lose valuable minutes/ seconds.

1. We use the experience as a teaching tool after the fact. Over a year later, François is still careful running down hills and says, "I don't want to split my chin open again!"

Chapter 5

"Is Today a Work Day or a Home Day, Mommy?"

We Were Here First

Alex

One morning back in mid-2008, while busy in the hustle and bustle of our morning routine, François quite calmly said, "I wish you were a 'home mom.' I don't like you going to work every day." Wow. I explained to him that I knew it was hard during the summer, but that in the fall he'd be so busy with school and after-school activities that we'd be getting home at about the same time. Not good enough; François pressed on, asking why I had to work. I tried to tell him that if I didn't work, we wouldn't have the money that I get for working, and that it goes toward things like food, our house and of course toys and clothes and all the fun trips we take together. He asked why Daddy couldn't work for the whole family. I explained that if Daddy were the only one working, we would never see him, much like friends of

ours where the husband leaves at 6 a.m. and gets home after
8 p.m., seeing their two young children only on weekends.
François pointed out that our investment banker neighbor
still gets home before his daughters are in bed. I countered
that the daughters are teenagers, go to bed much later and
often do their own thing at night, plus early on in his career
when they were little he likely worked much longer hours. I
added that as much as I would like staying home with him,
both Mommy and Daddy have to work plus it's something
that I enjoy, just as he enjoys going to school. I followed him
downstairs while the discussion continued, poured juice for
Johan and gave last-minute hand-off instructions to our
nanny. Simon sensed something was wrong and dragged
me into the bathroom, where I completely broke down, crying hysterically and hyperventilating. Sometimes you need
to just give up being strong for a minute or two, and in that
moment Simon understood that I needed to vent by crying,
which he let me do in a safe, child-free space.

Later that month, I was ready to resign from my job,
reverse Simon's vasectomy and have five more children.
In Ohio on a business day trip, all I wanted in the world
was to fly home on time so I could still put my boys to
bed. Instead of doing that, I was stuck in an airport ter-
minal because of bad weather. Just as we thought we were
cleared, John McCain, then desperately campaigning for
president, pulled his jet into our hangar—they were also
fighting the weather. The security caused our takeoff to be
bumped from 6:30 p.m. to 9:30 p.m. Then we got diverted
to Morristown, New Jersey and I finally crawled into the

house after 1 a.m. Even if I had been his greatest supporter, I would be mad. I love working, I really, really do, but my boys are more important.

At an Event Alex Threw for Second Time Around

Back then I worked full time for Victoria's Secret corporate in their New York office, keeping me away from home 50 hours per week and a lot more when I traveled. In early 2009 I was laid off, and when that happened, my first thought was to get the next office job I could. Working from home didn't occur to me until one day, a Facebook message led me to a designer consignment company, Second Time Around, that would become my first client. I saw an opportunity that could help both me and my family, and used the severance package from VS to go into business for myself. While I love being my own boss, one of the hardest things I've found about being a working mom is working from home. These days I work with a number of retail clients doing everything from graphic design to store fixtures to event planning. I can work from anywhere, which allows me to take care of my clients and also be able to participate in things I never could before, such as volunteering one day a week at school lunch and chaperoning field trips on occasion. We went from being a dual-nine-to-five-parent family where permission slips sometimes were forgotten, to a family where both parents contribute and school projects become a group activity.

It didn't happen overnight—the first summer was difficult. Still figuring out the work-from-home model, I would find myself hiding in the basement office (aka the bat cave) with the door closed, signing the kids up for any activity I could find or asking our nanny to take them to the park. A few times I found myself trying to work with the kids crowding around the computer asking to watch videos on YouTube of an octopus eating a shark or the Wiggles or a Batman made out of Legos. Now, between school, after-school activities and scheduling my work commitments with the kids in mind, I try as best I can to minimize the times I can't give them my full attention. They have also gotten used to me working at home, and know that when Mommy is on the computer, she's working and can't stop to play go fish, but she will when she's finished.

On that note I think children are capable of understanding quite a lot, which we grown-ups sometimes forget. When your children are busy, it helps them understand that you are busy, and sets them up to be effective individuals. As they grow older, another situation develops. They begin to be your allies in keeping the household peaceful. The boys are more likely (sometimes) to follow my direction to be quiet if I add that Daddy is sleeping, because they now know what it's like to be awakened by noise. I've overheard Simon telling François to "put down those high heels because Mommy will be cranky if she sees you wearing them." Cranky because of the noise, not that I'm worried he'll turn into a drag queen.

Simon

I was so fortunate that I was 20 years into my career when François was born, which meant that I'd passed the stage of working 70 plus hours and six days each week. I remember early on in my first marriage, when I was just launching my hotel finance career, that in addition to those 70 hours I was also at night school four nights each week. Putting in those hours both at work and school is no way to conduct a successful relationship let alone parenthood, at least not for me.

While I was always incredibly ambitious and held day dreams of being a millionaire by the time I was 25 no 3̶0̶ well make that 40… the reality is that I still must work for a living. However I am at a level where I can earn an incredibly good salary while only spending around 50 hours away from home each week, including my commute. After François was born I made a decision to slow down a little career-wise as I felt it more important to have a couple of extra hours a day with my son(s) than work extra hours to add thousands more on to my pay package. I was in the fortunate position that I was earning enough to make that decision. I know many can't, BUT I have also watched many dads, particularly in banking and law, who work incredibly long hours and whose time with their children is pretty much limited to weekends. It's now just over six years since François was born and the time really has flown. I can say that I would have missed an awful lot of fun watching François and then Johan develop if our time together had more or less been limited to non-working weekends. And not a day goes by when I regret the time we've had together.

Alex
Although I would never describe myself as a social conservative, I do believe in honoring relationship commitments. I believe that marriage should be allowed for everyone, gay and straight, and divorce should be difficult. Marriage is not disposable, and for that reason when the kids are about to drive you crazy you have to remember that you and your spouse were there first. We're very lucky that we're able to pay our nanny extra for two evenings a week to go out,

either just the two of us or with friends or to events around the city.

I think it's important to remember what we like to do, and make time to do it every once in a while. It may seem absolutely ludicrous when you are balancing one or more children and who knows what else in your life, but sometimes even a lost hour of sleep after the kids are in bed, spent reading a book, watching a movie or just talking with another adult is an investment in your sanity. I love to read, we both love opera, shopping and theatre, and Simon loves vegging on the couch watching tennis or golf while checking the cricket scores online. Simon and I love to take advantage of the new restaurants opening in our city constantly, and are big fans of tasting menus. We like to get dressed up in tuxes and ball gowns and sit in darkened opera houses while men and women sing beautiful, heart-wrenching music in front of gorgeous sets. The bottom line is this: whatever it is, be it facials once a month, bowling with the guys or underwater basket weaving, every happy parent I know has figured out what they need to maintain in order to stay "them," and work with their partners to make it happen. There's nothing worse than parents being so focused on the kids that there's no time left to nurture the relationship. Once the kids are grown, then what?

When we do spend time together away from the kids, we make sure the children are happy when we leave and have been very careful to choose caregivers we trust whose presence is also a treat for the boys.

Simon

Honestly the hardest thing about parenting in a city is not that we are in New York City, but that we are both thousands of miles from our own families. Alex's mom lives in Dallas, Texas, her two brothers in Texas and Kansas and my mum lives in Australia. I have two brothers also in Australia as well as a sister in Hungary. This has meant since day one that, apart from the occasional visit, we have had no local family support to fall back on. It's one of the reasons we decided with Johan's impending birth to hire a live-in au pair in lieu of having a mother or mother-in-law down the street or in the next suburb to call on.

Alex

We used to plan surprise trips for one another, which is more difficult with kids, but have channeled those ideas into more local fare. Eight and a half months pregnant with François, my 30th birthday was looming. We would normally do a tasting menu at a Michelin-starred restaurant complete with jewels and serenading (just kidding about the last bit, sort of), but at 37 weeks gone food was not particularly high on my list. What to do? Simon chartered a helicopter and for an hour or so we flew all around the city—over Central Park, over our apartment building, Yankee Stadium and the rest. Another time he chartered a yacht, complete with surprise party and private chef, as we sailed around the New York Harbor. We're lucky to live in a city where at any given moment you can find something to do that you've never done before. When planning Simon's 44th, I struggled for ideas. I'd thought of taking him to St. Barths for the weekend, but we'd been very busy at work and not seeing enough of the boys, etc. It wasn't a good time to go away. Instead, I got the boys involved in planning the festivities. François had recently discovered the joys of seeing a movie in a theatre—we have a great art house cinema on our corner with a brilliantly curated children's series twice a month. He suggested we have cake and goodies at home, then see a first-run film. With our nanny's assistance, the boys decorated the living room all afternoon. I ordered and picked up a cake from a bakery near my office and left work with just enough extra time to pick up the movie tickets, which for some reason weren't available online that day. What to buy someone you've known for almost 10 years? Rather than cufflinks, cologne or gadgets, I thought about things he loves but doesn't spend time on, and came up with music. These days it's rare for either of us to spend much time inside a music store, and frankly most are gone, along with the joy of browsing through racks and picking up actual CDs as opposed to downloading them. I selected a collection of the latest discs from his favorite artists, which was a hit. After our tea party at home with cake, the four of us went to see *Horton Hears a Who* (the boys' choice, of course!). Following the theatre, a friend of the family whom the boys adore was present at home to put them to bed, while Simon and I went out for a nice dinner at a restaurant we love.

Helicopter Mama, Three Weeks Before François' Birth

One thing Simon and I agreed upon when we decided to have children is that I would handle dirty diapers and related accidents, and he would handle vomit. As for merely wet diapers, whoever got there first changed them. Although he and I both have very strong stomachs and aren't squeamish, the one smell in the world that gets me is vomit—I just absolutely cannot stand it. Simon, on the other hand, isn't horribly fazed by it—his Achilles heel is feces in the various forms that come out of children's bottoms at appropriate and sometimes inappropriate times such as the middle of Thanksgiving festivities, while learning to use the toilet. It's not a hard-and-fast rule—neither of us would ever walk away from a child or a floor in need of clean up—but when we are both at home, it is a thoughtful division of labor. Example A: François throws up on the floor. Simon will swoop in, strip off the clothes and pick up the mess while I comfort F, clean his face and get him new clothes. Example B: While Johan learned to use the potty, we kept one in every room with wipes nearby. He was very good at getting himself there, but not so good at remembering to wipe up before repositioning underwear and trousers. He was also extremely invested in doing his part to keep the house clean and wanted to help by emptying his potty into the nearest toilet. Though if he couldn't find a toilet, sometimes a trash bin looked inviting... It was pretty much a constant race to keep an ear out for him using the potty in order to supervise wiping and make sure the contents actually got flushed. While I don't like the smell of poo either, it doesn't make me actually retch as it does Simon, so I am happy to take charge of that task.

Something else we did was unapologetically use the kids as an excuse to clean our emotional houses and we got rid of a few annoying people who weren't really friends. With so much going on in our lives I often feel like I barely have enough time to take care of myself, Simon and the kids, so I allow myself to not return those phone calls. I hardly have time to return my real friends' phone calls either, so I gave myself a break and either lost them as a friend, or not. (Any real friend reading this—I still love you!)

A bonus we hadn't counted on has been weight loss. As

I'd mentioned, Simon and I are huge food fans and never met a tasting menu we didn't like, plus we both love to cook. However, running around after two boys takes up enough of our time that we don't sit down to eat in the way we used to. Certainly we go out for meals, but it's much less likely that he or I will prepare a five-course meal at home with wines, etc. We do that only on occasion after the boys are in bed, as they don't appreciate grown-up food at all yet. I realized at one point that we no longer upheld a tradition of a cheese and meat platter upon returning home after work. The boys threw the cheese around and ate all the crackers, so I stopped putting it out, and we lost weight. We have also benefited from our desire to teach the boys about healthy eating. We don't allow soda or overly processed foods in the house, so we're not eating them either and everyone wins.

Sleep is something else that becomes almost as precious as our children. Simon and I alternate getting up on weekend mornings. Although for some reason he wakes early on the weekend, he tries to sleep in one day, and I sleep in the next or vice versa. Even if it's only to the ripe old hour of 8 a.m., it's still two hours more than we normally get, which is a bonus and makes the person who got extra sleep that much happier. The one who woke up early then takes a nap or gets free time later that day.

Partly due to the fact that in NYC there seems to be a nail bar on every corner, many women have perfect nails all the time here, or so it seems. It's as though there's somebody in a perfect little black dress whispering in your ear, "Don't let yourself slide, even for one little nanosecond. Make sure that even when the baby is crying, you comfort him or her while wearing a mud mask, bust-lifting lotion and hair softener. If you have boatloads of money, hire someone to hang around the house and when you fall asleep in a stupor with a kid on top of you, she can quietly give you a mani-pedi while not waking the ~~demon~~ baby. Have stylists come to your house and organize your closet by items that have the least amount of vomit on them." Yeah, right. I made a conscious decision not to worry about my hands, at the very least. It's not the $20 I mind, it's the hour spent walking in, getting a seat and waiting for the polish to dry, only to experience chips the next day. I do manage to use hand cream occasionally, and sometimes even body lotion (on good days). When an everyday product can do double duty such as Dawn Hand Renewal with Olay Beauty, a dish soap that seals in moisture while I'm tackling cleanup, sure, I'll buy it. Why stop there, could someone please come out with a fabric softener that moisturizes our legs inside our jeans? Bring on the shortcuts to make our lives easier. Is a manicure a shortcut? NO! I'm not willing to give up that time. My hands are soft and supple, but my nails aren't polished, and if you don't like it, don't look at them.

It may seem silly, but I know I feel more cheery when my legs are not hairy and I look presentable. Simon and I have both been really lucky that we are relatively fit, and with two young boys and a healthy diet we don't need to exercise much. Although it might seem old fashioned, we do make an effort to look halfway decent around the house. We never articulated this, but now that I think of it neither of us own sweatpants, nor do we lounge around in PJs. We get dressed immediately upon waking, and at home would be more likely to wear a slim pullover and jeans (Simon) or a casual dress (me). I think making a personal investment in the way you look pays off—it's absolutely true that I am nicer to Simon after he brushes his teeth, and I send myself reminders on my phone to get things like haircuts and waxes. I've also seen moms who aren't naturally thin, whether it's from the baby or genetics, but they still manage to put on makeup and a vomit-free shirt. They aren't trying to compete with Heidi Klum (neither am I) but are taking what they've got and working it. I love that.

Simon
While children had been the last thing on our minds when we married, neither of us could possibly imagine our lives without them now. That being said, we are also adamant that "we were here first" and we'd keep time for the two of us, an important part of our lives. This "us time" was never something we consciously set about planning but naturally evolved. I had fallen in love with Alex McCord the individual and while I loved her as a mom, too, I still wanted to spend some time with her alone. And so we'd go out together frequently whether to the theatre, the opera or a concert but also make sure that we'd eat out either before or after so we'd have some time to have a real conversation away from the distractions of work, home or family.

I really believe that this has contributed to keeping our marriage as strong as it is. We've been having our "date nights" long before we'd heard that term by getting out and spending time one on one. This keeps our relationship fresh. In the 10 plus years we've been together we've never had one of those awkward moments when a silence descends over the dinner table where we find ourselves struggling to find a topic of conversation. Yes, Alex and I were incredibly lucky to each find such compatible partners, but we've taken that luck and run with it and now as parents know that although it sounds such a cliché, "happy parents make happy kids."

Alex

Sometimes, despite all our stage-managing efforts, the kids win and we embrace that. One night while in St. Barths with the kids, we'd had a great night out. Late-afternoon cocktails in the capital with the kids playing around us, an early bite à deux followed by dinner with friends and finally dancing at Le Yacht. Our local babysitter that night was a friend we'd known for years as well and we chatted for a while upon our return. Finally, at about 3:30 a.m. we decided to cap the night off with a dip in the jacuzzi on the deck of our suite. As we went through to the deck we paused to admire our sleeping children and kiss them goodnight again. We hadn't made any undue noise while doing so, but no sooner had we turned on the jets when we heard a small voice behind us saying, "May I come in the jacuzzi, too?" We turned to see a beaming Johan, very pleased with himself that he'd gotten out of bed and followed the sound of our voices. At that point what could we say? We helped him out of his PJs and let him clamber in. He gave us big hugs and kisses and said, "We're a family in the jacuzzi!" It definitely ruined the moment Simon and I had been planning, but made room for one we'll never forget.

Jacuzzi!

TOP 10 THINGS WE DO BECAUSE WE WERE HERE FIRST:

10.   Take turns sleeping in on the weekend.

9.   If one of us needs to be somewhere after hours and we can't get a babysitter, the other will stay home with the kids.

8. We spend as much of our non-working time together as we can.

7. Surprise each other, even if it's just by cooking a favorite meal.

6. When we both worked in Manhattan we'd often try and meet on the subway coming home— gaining 20 minutes together.

5. Keep our "frustration radar" turned on. If one of us is about to crack at home, the other steps in to corral the kids.

4. We never, ever talk to the other when they are reading or checking game scores. Unless we're trying to stir up trouble.

3. Poke and prod each other to stay in touch with our friends.

2. We don't listen to people who have opinions on how we could run our relationship better. It works for us and that's all we need to know.

1. Have passionate sex. (Make love, but make sure you still !&#% each other, too!)

Chapter 6

I Saw Your Nanny... Being Normal?

Hiring Caregivers

From: SelfRighteousLady@SoapBox.com
To: Me@SaneParent.com
Subject: All the Things You're Doing Wrong

You have a bad child. You have a bad nanny, too. I hate my life and myself, so any time I have the opportunity to tear down other people's children and nannies, I will. Children should be seen and not heard. They should sit quietly on sofas while drinking water so as not to potentially stain the white couch. Nannies should never take their eyes off a child for one second. Actually having a nanny at all makes you a bad parent. Mothers should stay at home and knit toilet lid covers while keeping their children pristinely clean. There should never be visible mucous near their noses, nor should a child's clothes ever be dirty. If a kid has ice cream on their face, it means that they've had too much sugar and that no one cares about keeping them clean. They should be perfect, and if I ever see any behavior that isn't completely congruent to my standards, I'm going to run home and write about it on ISawYourNanny.com or whatever that self-righteous, nosey parker website is called.

Alex

OK, I made that up. But here's a real one—an e-mail from a parent at François' school:

From: "Concerned Parent"
To: Me
Subject: Re: Your Nanny

I just thought you should know that when your caregiver picks François up from school, she leaves Johan in the stroller at the bottom of the stairs. I felt obligated to stay with him until she returned.

On the surface this sounded dangerous, and I went straight to the school security guard the next day and asked about it. Turns out the stroller with Johan strapped into it was inside the gate, under the eyes of the school guard, who also had an eye on the other toddlers in their strollers at the bottom of the stairs.

I'm dating myself here, but do you remember the sit-com *Bewitched?* I used to watch reruns when I was about François' age and wished I could twitch my chin and make things fly. The nosey neighbor, Mrs. Kravitz, always snooped on Samantha Stevens and ran to tell her husband that something strange was going on. In the 21st century, the Mrs. Kravitzes of the world don't need to bother telling their husbands but can head straight to their computers to find a blog, any blog, that will welcome their rants. From the aforementioned ISawYourNanny.Blogspot.com to the hundreds of localized parenting bulletin boards or Yahoo or Google groups like ParkSlopeParents.com and BoCoCaParents, these boards, predominantly located in urban environments, are filled with overzealous (and bored?) Stay At Home Moms (SAHMS) who regularly report every little potential transgression of other children's caregivers.

Personally I think reading online nanny sightings is about as useful as hitting yourself in the head repeatedly. One thing I've learned recently is that cyberspace is an excellent dumping ground for negative energy: Internet posters use blogs and message boards as a way of getting out their own anger and frustration without attacking people they know in their everyday lives. Why would you trust an anonymous poster who describes your child and says that your caregiver was inattentive and chatting on the phone while the child played? Yes, I'm coming from the perspective that nothing terrible has ever been reported about any of my caregivers, and I suppose that it serves a function in that regard, however, shouldn't you have a bond of trust with a caregiver anyway? I've taken issue with other people's nannies exactly twice since we've had kids. Once, a nanny just seemed like she was venturing into the danger zone of being overtired and irritated, and was screaming at her charge when it didn't really seem warranted. I'd been near her in the park for 30 minutes. I asked her if she had an extra wipe, just to break the tension. It seemed to work, and she seemed not to have noticed my passive-aggressive intervention. Another time, also at the park, I reached into my stroller bag to discover that someone had stuffed the bag with copies of *Awake!* and some other Jehovah's Witness handouts. I asked the most likely suspect if she'd put them in my stroller. She answered, "Yes, can we talk about it?" No, thanks. I prefer my park visits without proselytizing.

We've been through several levels of childcare in the six and a half years we've been parents of children outside the womb. When François was a newborn we basically took him everywhere we went, and only left him for short bursts with friends. At 10 months, we started him two days a week in a private daycare, which we continued for a year until shortly before Johan's birth when we welcomed our first au pair.

Simon

Our international travel schedule was much greater (and easier) when we only had one child, and a couple of times a year we'd be in London on business. When François was around 11 months old we were staying in a hotel and needed a sitter for two separate occasions. On the first night, my ex-wife, Carol, was more than happy to look after François and so she came to our room, watched over a sleeping François while she ordered room service and demolished a half bottle of red wine. When we got back that night François was still sleeping and Carol wasn't far from needing to, too. We loaded her in a taxi, and the next night when we also needed another sitter, we couldn't use Carol as she was having dinner with us. This was in late 2004 and Craigslist had just launched in London and as such the few posts on it were mostly by American expats. So we perused the childcare postings and found a post-grad student who was studying in London for a year. We checked out her references from her previous childcare work in Connecticut both via e-mail and then by phone and confirmed her for that night. Wow, you may say that it is dangerous to hire an unknown expat to look after one of life's greatest possessions, but is it anymore dangerous than getting a sitter through the hotel (like we had done previously in Morocco)?

Alex
Morocco? Ha! We took François with us when he was five weeks old and hired a babysitter through the hotel for the couple of hours we couldn't take him to events with us. It was a company retreat for Simon and most of the planned family activities were fine for a baby, but there were a couple of cocktail parties and a dinner where I couldn't avoid needing childcare. The young lady was a local student, and the only common language we spoke was French. She managed to overfeed him all the pumped milk I'd left her in the first hour, and instead of calling me,

rang down to room service for cow's milk. That night we learned he wasn't allergic! The next night, after solving the milk situation by giving her a feeding schedule and a tin of formula just in case, I still managed to learn another, somewhat delayed lesson. If you leave your backup cell phone in the room, lock it in the safe. The following month after receiving a huge bill, it took three calls to our cellular provider to explain why I had several hours worth of phone calls to an unlisted number in Saudi Arabia.

Bar Tabac Brunch with Au Pair Rosa

There is no one perfect solution to childcare, and it's true that it takes more than just the parents to raise a child. We were very happy with the daycare we chose to begin with but weren't sure how we'd like the au pair program.

Basically you have someone come and live with you for a year, or potentially two years if you apply for an extension, though we never took advantage of that. Au pairs normally wind up in the program during a gap year between high school and college, or college and grad school, and are between the ages of 18 and 26. They can be from any country with which the U.S. has diplomatic relations and it is seen as a cultural and educational exchange with a requirement that the au pair complete a certain number of college courses during her stay. That's the official version. In the handbook they don't tell you what to do when the au pair comes into your bedroom in the middle of the night crying because she feels sick, or how to console a teenager who can't perform her babysitting duties because she's upset about something her boyfriend posted about her on Facebook.

The positives about having an au pair are that in a best-case scenario she becomes a member of the family. We could set the work schedule weekly and with a good household relationship there was opportunity for last-minute flexibility when we needed it. A young caregiver has lots of energy and the ability to keep up with two active boys, and is relatively malleable and mentally able to adapt to the childcare style of the parents. With all the visa paperwork handled by the agency, traveling abroad with an au pair is drama-free as long as she remembers her passport! A young au pair enjoys running around in the park and throwing balls, marauding through street fairs and blowing bubbles. The negatives are that you wind up parenting the au pair as well, that the condition of the house reflects that a teenager lives in it, and you may come home to find them borrowing your clothes, watching *Gossip Girl* with your toddlers and downloading naughty pictures onto their computers during off hours—we learned quickly to keep the au pair's computer separate from our household network after accidentally opening a video of her with her boyfriend we just really, truly did not need to see. Bring on the brain bleach! Sometimes we'd run into food issues—lots of teenagers love soda and candy, and it's difficult to have that around a child without being cajoled into giving them "just one taste." We did make it a household rule that our au pairs couldn't eat junk food on duty, and gave them a mini fridge in their room for contraband. What wound up being crucial for us when hiring au pairs was meeting the candidate in advance to be sure we were on the same page. We participated in the program for three years—the first year we met the father and a cousin, the second year we met the au pair and her mother, and they came to our house and the final year all interviewing was conducted over the phone. That last year was the only year we had a problem. Of course no year was perfect and there were always little ups and downs—over the three years I'd say that our biggest difficulties were to do with sharing our home with a teenager and dirty dishes and laundry being left around. The final year, however, there were serious cultural issues.

The direct translation of au pair is "on par" or equal to, and an au pair is meant to be treated as a member of the family. We went out of our way to make sure this happened during all three years including taking them with us on weekend trips, subscriptions to French cable TV, concert tickets and evenings out, but the final year we had a girl who just wasn't a good fit. She was sullen, melodramatic and kept a blog about how she hated Americans, hated France, hated us and the children but loved New York. I think she must have thought we were idiots, and when she asked to leave early we were only too happy to get her out of our home. Unfortunately that experience soured us on the whole program, but after three years we were also more than ready to have a caregiver who didn't live with us. We replaced her with our housekeeper/relief nanny, who up until that point had been coming in one day per week for over a year, and who is still with us.

Alex:	Our au pair is going back to France early.
François:	Is she coming back?
Alex:	No, she's not.
François:	Good. May I have her room?

We've been lucky to keep our nanny since then, though now the chums are both in school full time and we don't need her as much as we used to. Since she doesn't work 40 hours per week anymore, we picked a schedule everyone could live with and keep it sacred for everyone's sanity.

We've seen what happens when friends of ours keep their caregivers around the clock—at some point even the extra pay doesn't seem worth it. Given that our crazy schedules sometimes change at the last minute, we've cultivated a list of relief babysitters. Some of our resources have included a former au pair who returned to NYC for school, the high school-aged neighbors on our street, single friends who enjoy playing with kids, my cousin's son who moved to Williamsburg and plays in a band, etc. As the boys grow up, we enjoy bringing in male babysitters when we can, which comes with another set of issues. Guys are great with playing foosball and riding bikes in the park; not so great with making beds and getting the little beasts bathed. We've come to accept that tradeoff and the boys love it when they can have a playdate with a big boy. A former boyfriend of a relative of mine lives a few blocks away and is in grad school—Simon and I recently left the boys in his care and as we went out the door they were happily playing guitar and spraying each other with Mr. Clean in the garden. Perfect! (Note to potentially horrified readers: they weren't actually spraying each other with undiluted cleaner. Ever since François could walk and talk, he's been kind of obsessed with the animated Mr. Clean. That didn't bother me at all because I am obsessed with Mr. Clean as well, even more so now that the new disinfecting bath spray comes with the freshness of Febreze, knocking out germs and smells of boys' feet. I told you I was obsessed— didn't believe me, did you?) When anyone would spray a surface, he'd desperately want to help. I took to saving a bottle or two with the label intact and filling with plain water. He'd proudly walk around saying, "Now I'm Mr. Cleaner." But I digress.

Regardless of whether the caregiver is an au pair, a nanny or a backup babysitter, one question often asked during interviews is, "Do you use a nanny-cam?" I prefer to hire someone I can trust implicitly and then leave them to it—I couldn't imagine having a camera set up where I'd watch the children every hour. For one thing, I wouldn't be able to concentrate on work, and for another, where is the trust? At work I've never looked over the shoulder of anyone who reports to me, so why would I do so with the caregiver of my children? I've always said, don't drug them or hit them, report any accidents or fighting at the end of the day and keep them from running into traffic. Allow a maximum of one hour of TV per day and make sure they go outside unless the weather is bad. Beyond that, it's up to them. Confidence in your caregiver breeds confidence in their care of the children. I love it when shopkeepers in our neighborhood refer to us as François and Johan's parents. From a very early age and from Johan's birth, they would patrol the streets of Cobble Hill with their caregivers, and around the age of three some locals began calling François the Mayor of Cobble Hill.

Sometimes I really wish we had family living near us. Although we schedule regular chats via video with our more technologically advanced relatives, the others miss the day-to-day little things like Johan singing "Hit the Road, Jack," or an art project the boys created together. It's also impossible to get Grandma over to babysit if Mom and Dad need to go out for 45 minutes. To that end, we've made our own family, whether it's with childless friends who want to borrow some for an afternoon, or friends who have kids of similar ages and want to get them together for drop-off playdates. When it's just for an afternoon, four kids can be easier to watch than two, as they have a ball playing and the novelty of being together is fresh.

TOP 10 THINGS CAREGIVERS HAVE INADVERTENTLY DONE TO AMUSE, ANNOY OR THRILL US:

10. Put cheese away in the freezer while talking to the boys.

9. Accidentally used a household cleaning wipe when changing a diaper. Johan did not notice.

8. Let baby François lick the edge of a shot glass of vanilla rum on vacation. He wanted more and tried to grab the bottle!

7. Get into our backyard blow-up pool fully clothed because she didn't have a swimsuit.

6. Obsessively boil every dish baby Johan used, and made François put on gloves when holding him.

4. Offered to take the boys out for dinner and asked them where they wanted to go. (First mistake.) Our enterprising young men directed him to an upscale French bistro and ordered $60 worth of pasta and hot chocolate. Yes, we paid him back.

3. Spent hours helping the boys make homemade, glitter-filled photo collages for Simon's and my birthdays—we still have them!

2. Really "get" the working-from-home model, and help enforce it in kid-friendly terms.

1. When a former caregiver told several neighborhood parents and nannies that we were awful people, unprompted, her replacement loyally told everyone the truth and to consider the source.

Chapter 7

"Putting To Death Is Not Nice," a Duet for Two Boys and a Guitar

Lessons Learned by Boisterous Children

Alex

It cracks me up when people expect children to be perfectly well behaved all the time. Quite honestly, why should they be? We adults aren't. Many adults treat each other horribly on a regular basis, and I would rather have a boisterous boy running around me with a drippy paintbrush, than a superior kid sitting still and saying nasty things about her frenemy. In many ways kids are feral animals, and at the end of each day if there's no blood and no ruined furniture, we've won.

About four months ago we came home one weekend afternoon to find the boys madly playing their guitars and running around. Our friend and their honorary godfather, Sava, was on the sofa howling with laughter and we eagerly asked him what had happened. Sava said, "François, come and sing your song for Mommy and Daddy." Both boys happily launched into a song that basically involved screaming, "Putting to death is not nice, killing isn't good!" over and over while rocking out with their guitars and throwing their heads around. I'm still not sure what inspired the song, although Sava did confirm that nothing had been put to death, but I fully agree that in any case it is not nice. They've begun protesting the death penalty early.

The boys understand the basics—i.e., no killing. No breaking things, no punching in the face (unless your brother really, really annoys you). When you get to the finer points of appropriate behavior it's frustrating to not be able to make yourself understood. We went through a big learning curve when the boys were between two and three years old. Once they are able to communicate with you using words, it's tough to not open the floodgates and bombard them with information, but we had to stop ourselves because it just wasn't sinking in. Though I'm a very verbal person to begin with, it's unbelievably annoying to explain why pouring mustard sauce in the toaster will break it, why dropping Daddy's best watch would mean that Daddy could never wear it again, why there's no eating yogurt on the suede sofa despite their promise to be very careful and on and on. Although they could speak and understand, at that age they still couldn't communicate anything approaching an adult level, and we finally learned to save our breath, or at least put it on pause for a few years. We admitted that training kids was rather like training animals—reward for good behavior and physically prevent the bad behavior. I still do try a short explanation each time, but if it doesn't work I move on to the next option.

What works best for us 90 percent of the time is a three count, followed by a time-out if the behavior hasn't stopped. For example, if François is holding a coloring book over his head and not giving it to Johan, he has a three count to give it back, otherwise it's a time-out. When an action is destructive or dangerous, we skip the counting and go directly to a time-out: if Johan hits François, it's an automatic time-out and vice versa. A third permutation is when there's a behavior that has to stop immediately, say if Johan has a big blue indelible marker and is running through a white hotel suite. I swoop in and grab the marker as to risk a three count would be to risk decoration of the sofa. Neither of us is above scaring the daylights out of either of them with a well-placed growl or shout, and yes, when necessary we have spanked them both and will again.

Sometimes I get angry that people mock our perceived lack of discipline of our children on the show, when in reality on the streets of Brooklyn with no cameras around, we're a hell of a lot stricter than most parents. We've discovered that when dealing with the boys on the show it's just not possible to please everyone. If we are too strict there will always be someone to be critical and if we're not, then another set call us overly permissive. It's definitely a case of damned if you do and damned if you don't! Yes, we do sometimes want to set our hair on fire and yes, the boys can be rowdy. We also high-five each other when we pick up the kids and the grown-up delivering them goes on about how well-behaved and mature they were. We take the good with the bad. No one is perfect—everyone is interesting.

Our goal is to raise children who are intelligent and productive. We want them to be inquisitive, confident, have empathy for others and a strong moral compass. It's useful for them to know the social graces, such as not to chew with their mouths open, not to be boorish or eat or drink to excess and to have a firm handshake. I don't particularly care whether they are considered "nice" or "popular," although those qualities are good, too. Ultimately if my boys are gainfully employed and happy, that's all that matters. I want to see them excited by life and all it has to offer, not passively sitting by so that they won't offend anyone. I want to raise my children more or less in the way our parents raised us.

One of my first memories of being wrangled as a kid was at our vacation home in St. Thomas—this would have been in the late '70s. Our house was on a cliff and was sort of donut-shaped with a pool in the middle, and on that afternoon a fabulous poolside cocktail party was in force. Amidst the jollity, my three teenaged brothers decided a fabulous addition to the festivities would be to put on a show for the guests by diving off the roof of the house into the pool. Dad or someone took a great photo of my brother Paul standing on the roof, arms spread wide, ready to plunge. Someone else chuckled and said, "Don't break your neck." Meanwhile I was determined to steal the food from and pull the tail of the long-suffering German Shepherd who belonged to our next-door neighbors. For some reason I always thought he should eat apples with me, instead of his dog food, and was prepared to enforce the issue. "Croix, if she annoys you just bite her," someone said to the dog. He never did, patient dog that he was, but I got the point. They say that girls play "let's have a tea party" and boys play "let's jump off the roof." There's a photo of me somewhere playing "let's have a tea party *on* the roof," so between Simon and me we have passed on rather boisterous genes to our children.

Alex and Dad on Ladder

Simon

I am a great believer in letting one's children learn the hard way. And while it's always good to learn from others' mistakes, we all have our own to learn from, too.

One night when I was around 11 years old my mum was out and I was in bed. I am sure my brother, six years my senior, was around, but my memory of this night doesn't recall. What I do recall though, is as clear as if I had just watched it on video. I crawled out of bed and put my clothes on over my pajamas and left the house, walking out onto the street. At the time we were living on the outskirts of a small town in Australia with cane fields bordering our back fence. Our street was lined with houses but backed by farms. It was semi-rural and also a dead-end, as the bridge had been washed out years ago and was never repaired. As such, it was a pretty safe area and this was 1975. Anyway I picked up my golf club and as I wandered down the street, I saw my first cane toad of the night. This particular toad had been introduced into Australia in the '30s to eradicate the cane beetle, which was damaging cane crops, however it was less successful at that than it was as multiplying at an alarming rate. As a result, I had only ever known it as a pest and vermin. No different to how an NYC kid regards rats.

These toads secret a poison (stored behind their eye in the parotid gland) as part of their defense against predators and my 11-year-old brain understood that this poison, if it got in my eyes, could cause blindness. As I raised my golf club back over my head and swung it forcefully forward, the toad took a slight step. Instead of catching its body dead center and sending it 100 yards down the bitumen road, I caught its face, causing its parotid glands to rupture and spray my face with their contents.

Scared and petrified, I raced home, madly rinsed my eyes with water and as I crawled back up to my top bunk, I remember glancing at the ceiling and thinking that that would be the last thing my eyes would ever see.

Sometime throughout the next afternoon I suddenly remembered that I was *supposed* to be blind and was elated to know that I clearly wasn't. But what this experience did teach me was that if I was meant to be somewhere, then there I would be. There was no more sneaking out of the house after that.

Alex

My dad was in the oil business, and around the time I started school he bought several fields in rural southeast Kansas. I spent my school years there and we traveled during vacations. In the oil fields there were lots of fascinating pieces of equipment to play on and with, and although Dad would sometimes explain what the machinery did, more often than not he'd just let me explore. I remember getting filthy on a regular basis, climbing up and down trucks outfitted with all sorts of barrels and pulleys and although they were never far away, I had plenty of room to fall down if I didn't hold on tight. My parents believed in taking responsibility for your own personal space pretty early on and learning consequences and that is something I'm trying to pass along to my kids. I once found a small snake in the field and brought it in to show Mom, who happened to be washing her hair over the tub at the time. The guilt I felt at her hitting her head on the tap and hurting herself because of me was worse than any time-out, spanking or removal of privileges she could have imposed. Another time I had adopted a small turtle I'd found in the field, and after a few days of feeding and taking care of it, I put him in one of my mother's handbags. Needless to say he died in there, and it wasn't necessary to impose an additional punishment. I'd been upset that I thought I'd lost him and couldn't find him. Then Mom got out that handbag, found the body and had to throw away the purse because the smell had permeated the material. I couldn't believe I'd forgotten the turtle, was responsible for its death and of course the mini-fashionista in me was also upset I'd caused Mom to lose a favorite bag.

I had a moment of déjà vu last year in the kitchen and realized at least part of me has indeed turned into my mother. Johan and François were capering around the kitchen while I made pasta for dinner, and François was in "Let's badger Mommy" mode. The F-Bomb wanted to put his hands in the pasta water. "No, that's getting hot." "Mommy, I want to dooo it, I'm going to dooooooo it." After about 10 rounds of this, he pulled a chair over next to me and continued the chant down the back of my neck. I could think of a thousand retorts, I could easily scoop him up and put him in his room for a time-out. Maybe not this time. He had been playing this game pretty much any time a pot was on the stove, and we were all getting sick of it and this time I was sure that the water was hot enough to shock without scalding him. In anticipation of him plunging his hand in, I turned the flame off, reached over to the freezer, got out an ice pack and stepped aside. François looked at me, looked at the water, looked at me again and put a finger in. A second later he was on the counter with his ice pack and a piece of ice to suck on for good measure. I'm still not 100 percent sure whether a similar experience happened to me as a kid or whether I had a dream that I would do this someday, who knows. In any case, François has never done it again.

While writing this paragraph a short person begins breathing down my neck…

François: Why did I want to stick my hands in boiling water?

Alex: Very good question—I think because I told you not to.

François: Why did you let me do it?

Alex: Because you kept asking and wouldn't stop!

François: Can I put my hands in boiling water now?

Alex: Sure, go ahead. You'll need to boil some first. Want me to help you?

François: HAHAHAHHAHA, Mommy.
(Runs away cackling maniacally.)

Simon

Having grown up in a single-parent household, my mum was the only parent available for discipline. Sometimes there'd be times where, rightly or wrongly, one of my two brothers or I would be a little too much of a handful for my mum to discipline. Accordingly there were occasions when she enlisted the aid of a family friend, an honorary uncle. And thus we came to learn about "Captain Thunderbolt" the large, wizened and calloused right hand of said uncle. This right hand, whose palm would very occasionally be whipped across my clothed buttocks, was named after Fred Ward, a Bushranger renowned for committing over 200 crimes in six and a half years across the northern part of New South Wales, where we were living at the time.

Both François and Johan have also learned to be wary of "Captain Thunderbolt" and the mere mention of his name particularly when my palm is held upright, provides sufficient warning to them to stop their concurrent transgression.

Alex

Probably the hardest disciplinary thing for me as a parent is consistency. Simon and I have different levels of tolerance for noise, running and flailing, and sometimes we butt heads over where the line in the sand should be. If I'm copywriting or designing something on my laptop, the world can literally be ending around the desk and I'll keep on going. It's the same for Simon if he's dialed into the hotel from his PC. Actually, when either one of us is working from home on the computer, the kids could be stringing up the cats on a spit and we wouldn't notice. The temporarily-disconnected-from-the-computer parent is typically trying to do laundry, tidy up the kitchen, organize paperwork or something generally not fun and tends to resent the parent on the computer. I'm particularly guilty of this and wind up with a much shorter fuse than normal for boyish behavior.

Bear Cubs

Simon

Personally whether at work or at home I could gladly go without exacting discipline, however, it seems that as we learn limits by stretching parameters as far as we are allowed, discipline is required. So whether we fall off after we've gone too far or get told off before we've fallen, either way we learn. And such is the way with children. From birth they've been pushing the limit of their surroundings, which is why many parents buy physical barriers to stop their children falling and injuring themselves. However sometimes a verbal scolding or more is called for and it is in this area where Alex and I most differ as parents. Like many instances of parenting I do think that we each parent in certain ways either because of or despite the way in which we ourselves were parented. I remember when Francois was very young Alex would get annoyed with me if I tried to reason with him when I was trying to stop him doing such and such: "He doesn't understand. A simple 'no, don't do that' should suffice," she'd say. As Francois got older slight disagreements would occur, but one thing where we never disagreed was that we wouldn't air our disagreements about our disciplining in front of the children. If one of us didn't like the way the other handled something, we'd go along with it at the time and discuss it afterwards.

Alex

As they grow, it's funny to watch the boys play off one another. If François gets into trouble, the J-Boy will sidle up to me and say, while casting a superior glance at his big brother, "Mommy, I'm being a good boy" or, "*I don't need a* time out!" Likewise, if François gets fed up with Johan not sharing his toys, he'll try to send his little brother to his room. Another thing we've noticed as they have become better able to communicate is that they've both tried lying, as most kids seem to do. I remember from my own childhood that sometimes I lied about silly things because I didn't want a grown-up to be angry that I'd done, or not done, something. Because of that I've relentlessly told the boys to "cop to it," whatever *it* may be. As they mature I've tried to explain to them that lying about something makes it worse, and have at the same time tried to be lenient whenever they bravely tell me about something they've screwed up. It's a work in progress, but I like the progression.

Two Pals in a Tub

Thing 1:	Mommy, he hit me!
Me:	You need to tell your brother "sorry."
	Right now.
Thing 2:	No, I didn't hit him.
Me:	Are you kidding me? I saw you!
Thing 2:	No, you didn't.
Thing 1:	Are you both blind?
Me:	Simmer down, both of you!

TOP 10 THINGS WE NEVER THOUGHT WE WOULD HAVE TO EXPLAIN:

10. Why hot pizza stones do not like Legos.

9. Why "I'm going to chop your feet off" is not an appropriate response to your brother, who won't put his shoes on.

8. Why gluing pages of New York magazine together cannot be undone.

7. If you stick your hand in a cat's mouth, she will bite it.

6. If you try to put your parents in time-out, guess where you end up?

5. If you throw your fire engine into the East River, Daddy is not going in after it.

4. At bedtime if you suddenly announce that your homework isn't finished, too bad for you. Mommy will not ask the teacher for more time.

3. That if you tell your brand new babysitter that Mom and Dad always let you stay up until 10 p.m. and eat ice cream, he won't believe you.

2. Why you can't bring your potty out and use it on the floor in the middle of a dinner party. (A certain two-year-old tried.)

1. It's not OK for a kid to call a grown-up a mother****er, even if it's the truth.

Chapter 8

Don't Listen to the Well-Meaning Morons

The 1,001 Things We're Doing Wrong

"You're pregnant? When are you guys moving home and will it be Dallas, Kansas or Australia?" – A Midwestern transplant who always shuddered at the idea of anyone raising kids in the city and who has since moved to Indiana.

You might not like the city, pal, but it IS home for us. We wouldn't dream of leaving!

"My daughter is perfect. Her table manners are excellent, she never speaks unless spoken to and we've always had white sofas at home since she was a child, with no staining." – A woman with one preteen daughter, no sons.

Your daughter sounds boring. I wouldn't want my sons to date her.

"You're not bringing *that* in here are you?" – A snarling host at a normally child-friendly restaurant.

If by that you mean the stroller, no, I'm going to fold it up and put it in the coat check. If you mean the baby, perhaps you should work somewhere else. I know in the city particularly there are lots of people who don't like kids and think the stroller brigade has taken over the neighborhood, but all I want is a bowl of pasta. I promise I won't bring my breasts out.

"My children have to adapt to my life, not the other way around." – A pregnant mother-to-be.

The last time I saw her, with her five-month-old, she'd cut her hair off and spent the entire evening doing everything she said she'd never do.

"I cannot believe you are outside your house with a 48-hour-old baby." – A father of five, who I'm not sure has ever changed a diaper.

Pardon me, but where else should I be? If none of us are sleeping, why not take a walk?

"Don't take your baby on the subway. He needs earplugs or his eardrums will burst." – A crazy old bat on the subway with badly applied red lipstick, who carried a huge handbag, probably containing supplies for every possible contingency she could imagine.

I should have asked her whether she was wearing earplugs.

"Why are you outside?" – A bagel seller in Montreal, in February.

I'm hungry and the stroller is well protected under the plastic cover. Johan is warm and cozy, the others are asleep in the hotel and I'm going stir-crazy. Is that enough, or should I buy my bagel from someone else?

"Why isn't your baby wearing a hat? Where is his hat?"
– A heavyset Russian woman sitting next to us on a flight to London, when the temperature inside the aircraft was stiflingly hot.

If we were in Russia, I'd wear a hat, too. But we're not. We're on an airplane and it's bloody hot.

"Did you know your child has a runny nose?" – A lady in line at a coffee shop.

Wow, I had no idea. I have one, too. Thanks for being too polite to point that out.

"Excuse me, your baby is crying." – Someone said to Simon as they peered into the stroller to try and determine the cause of said noise.

You don't say! Do you think, you stupid idiot, that I don't hear that? Do you think I think it's just loud music? Do you think I don't want him to stop and that I like it???

"Take your baby out of the car seat! Put his chest on your skin! Skin to skin contact is best!" – A benevolent grandma to Simon on a bitterly cold day on the subway.

That may well be, but it's impractical on the subway, particularly when both Simon and François were wearing coats and getting off at the next stop.

"Babies can't ride camels." – A skeptical Sherpa in the desert.

OK, I'll go along with that one. We tried and François was not amused.

"You flew with your baby at 13 days old? What kind of a parent are you?" – A newlywed who said in the same breath that she was waiting to be told by her husband when the time was right to start a family.

One who travels and takes my baby with me.

"Your child probably has ADHD—you should get him tested." – A generally mouthy woman with no boys.

For God's sake, lady, just because a five-year-old doesn't look you in the eye, hold still and shake your hand doesn't mean he needs medication. He's five. Get a grip.

Alex
In my opinion, child-rearing is something you figure out as you go along, and it's really subjective and instinctual. As long as the kids are safe, what goes on is really up to the parents. Everyone has different levels of tolerance for children and the noises, messes and situations they bring, and I remind myself of this often, particularly when my own head whips around at the sound of a wailing baby. Sometimes I feel like I should offer to help, other times ignore it or occasionally

think about sending the afflicted parents over a round of drinks. It's exacerbated in the city because we're all in such close contact with one another. In a suburban area you can retreat to the inside of your house or car and not have much interaction with anyone. In the city you are forced to deal with people just to go about your daily business, and when you walk to the supermarket, get on the bus or the subway or try to hail a cab, people will see you and your children. Not only will they see whatever heaven or hell you might be enduring at the moment, they will be close enough to offer running commentary, and in New York particularly no one is afraid to tell you what they think you're doing wrong. There are so many neurotic, short-tempered people in this city, and often they came from somewhere else and have dreamy, bucolic memories of growing up playing in fields, far removed from places where children are tempted to lick the credit card machines in the back of taxis.

The thing is, everyone—and I mean everyone—will offer an opinion about what they think you should be doing better as a parent. This is especially unhelpful when offered by someone without youngsters in tow. If they don't have a two-year-old boy right now, chances are they don't know or don't remember what it's like to tell one why he can't jump onto the subway tracks while you soothe the six-week-old strapped to your chest. When I hear people make comments about my parenting skills or my boys, I first take a look at who is talking. If it's someone with a couple of young children, I will listen more readily than if it's a child-less woman or someone with an older only child. At one point, we lived in a nine-unit co-op apartment building, and there were two newborn babies in the building, one of whom was François. People in the building liked to gossip about us even before the birth, as they thought we weren't team players. They didn't like it that we insisted on getting city permits for building work instead of hiring Lefty the unlicensed handyman who looked like he'd just walked off the set of *The Sopranos*, didn't like the way we did our 2002 renovation, didn't like anything about us, really. I was amazed, however, to go up the stairs one night and overhear a group of the women discussing my parenting! They felt I was too strong and stringent with sleep training, which made me laugh because if anything, we were constantly getting up each night for a while. I overheard one say, "I'm not saying she's not a good parent… but," and at that point I had to laugh at myself for eavesdropping, turned around and continued up the stairs. None of those women had ever had a baby, whether it was by choice, they weren't ready yet or weren't able to. To them, any cry whatsoever probably signified World War III. I decided to let the jackals cackle and go on about my business.

Anytime I want to slap an annoying parent I remind myself that they are in the same boat as me—they are trying to do the best they can for their children, and are often worn out, feel they aren't putting in a full day either at work or at home and feel overwhelmed. Guess who the easiest target might be to vent frustration? Other parents, of course. How many times have we been on the playground and witnessed a mother, father or caregiver snipe at another, often for little reason at all. Recently I heard a mother at the playground threaten her son with skipping a birthday party if he didn't share a plastic car. A nearby nanny smirked, "Good luck sticking to that, honey." I have to admit, I agreed with the nanny on that one. One of my biggest challenges is to set consequences that are major enough but easily enforceable. My other challenge is to not jump on that same judgmental soapbox. Last year I went with a friend and all our children (four in total) to work on a Father's Day project for our husbands. There was a mom at another table who wore all black and told her hyperactive daughter that they had to have a family meeting to decide what to do next. The type of woman who might ask her daughter to "process her feelings" about which color to choose. The type of woman who wanted make a big huge hairy deal about *including* her daughter in the decision-making process and "negotiating" the next best step for the family to take in the pottery shop. Pardon me while I shoot myself. Judgy Wudgy was a bear. Judgy Wudgy did not care. But seriously, around so many breakables and so much permanent paint my instinct was to do whatever was in my power to keep our four kids at the table and not demolishing things we'd have to pay for or painting their neighbors. I didn't feel the need to call a meeting about it.

Releasing frustration can happen in person or online. There are many websites out in cyberspace that cater to new parents, some of which are interactive discussion boards, and the dialogue can be downright scathing. One I used to surf regularly was Urban Baby. Back in 2003 when I was pregnant with François, I logged on and was amazed. After

I sifted through the acronyms (DCs = Darling Children, DS and DD = Darling Son or Daughter, CIO = Cry It Out and on and on), I was shocked to see the aggression put forth. One poster asked a question about formula and mentioned in her post that she did not want to breast-feed. Several people responded that she was a horrible mother for not wanting to nurse, one even suggesting that women who did not want to nurse should have their children taken away from them. Huh? I thought people logged on to these websites for support, not to be told they're idiots who can't parent their children properly. Case in point, one comment: "I am a Stay at Home Dad and need advice. When did you toss the pacifier?" Response #1: "Stay at Home Dads are pathetic." Response #2: "Six months, loser. If you stay home, why don't you know this?" Response #3: "If you don't know that, time to man up and get a job." Come on, people, that's just rude. There's lots of discussion about crying it out, the process of leaving your child in the crib to settle themselves, usually throughout the night but sometimes during naps, too. Ferberizing is another term, named for a Dr. Ferber who wrote a book about it. Anyone who posts on a message board who is in favor of CIO thinks the opposition is too airy-fairy and permissive. Those against CIO think the others are abusive parents. We stopped somewhere in the middle and realize that it's a highly personal decision—we wouldn't condemn a mom or dad for leaping out of bed at every peep during the night, or from walking away at 8 p.m. and not coming back until 6 a.m. regardless of the screams. If they want to hit either sleep training extreme, fine—it's not hurting me and I feel no need to suggest in an online forum they're either killing themselves and their relationship or somehow harming their child.

Three Boys Sleeping

Simon
These forums most seem to satisfy the insecure mom (IM) or occasionally dear husband (DH), who gladly attack the original poster (OP) as a way to make them feel better about their own deficiencies and insecurities as parents. I am amazed at the number of seemingly intelligent moms who populate these sites and the vitriol that they happily unleash on fellow moms. They say that hell has no fury like a woman scorned, whereas for the 21st century surely hell no longer hath fury, as it's all been hurled at the belittled and scorned Internet mom.

Alex

Ultimately, I think we all have to realize that there is no one right way to parent children. Not only that, styles of parenting that work can change from sibling to sibling. Johan will take a nap if he's led to a quiet place and told he needs one. He will only put on the shirt you want him to in the morning when bribed with bagels. François, on the other hand, doesn't ever, ever want to sleep, but will happily try on not only his shirts but anyone else's as well. While Johan is a pickier eater than François, he will busily clean up his toys in order to make room for a new project. François usually needs to be shocked with a cattle prod (or at least the threat of a time-out) in order to straighten up the minefields he creates in his room. Oh, and guess what else? Sometimes the kids flip-flop—one night François simply kissed us good night and nodded off, while Johan screamed, cried and insisted on his door being open and the hallway light left on. Inconsistency, thy name is child.

A mom came up to me recently and said, "I know you don't like TV in kids' rooms, but I had to do it." In order to get their child out of the parents' bed, they allowed the two-year-old to watch a calming baby video in her own room each night, which resulted in the child being willing to climb into her own bed and made for much more rested and happier parents. Who could argue with that? Whatever works best for your family is the right decision to make, and if chatty neighbors don't like it, screw 'em.

This is not to say that those whose children are grown don't know what they're talking about. Far from it. Some of the best advice I've received over the years has been from grandparents, possibly because they've had time to put it all into perspective and not get too worked up about the small stuff.

"He's not sick or wet. He's just mad. Let him vent." – My mom.

"If you're going out to a cocktail party that ends at 8 p.m., let the boys stay up until 8:30 so you can put them to bed yourself." – A prominent socialite who to my knowledge has never been on TV.

"Pumping's hard work. The fact that you got anything while you're on a business call, on the coldest day of the month so far, is an achievement." – Simon's mum, whose words of encouragement helped me relax and pump another four ounces.

All advice aside, sometimes what really helps us is laughing. Once at a rather hoity-toity wedding, six-month-old François started to get fussy. As I glanced nervously around to see whether people could hear him, an old dear at our table put down her martini, rummaged in the stroller and triumphantly retrieved his pacifier, stating, "His stopper fell out," and unceremoniously plugged it back into his mouth. Stopper. Ha! 'Cause it makes him STOP. Another night when a jet-lagged friend had just returned from Greece and stopped over for a nightcap, teething Johan woke up and set off toddler François and soon they were both screaming. My friend calmly said, "Right. Scotch or tequila?" It took me a second to confirm she wanted to pour it for us, not them.

TOP 10 WAYS WE MAKE OURSELVES FEEL BETTER WHEN IT'S ALL GETTING TO BE TOO MUCH:

10. Check to see whether the person offering advice has children. How old are they?

9. Do they have a point? Are they right? It is entirely possible.

8. Will we ever see this person again? If not, can we get away with unleashing our fury on them? Note, if you're reading this and decide to try it yourself, go big or go home.

7. Go online and read stories of parents who lost a child at birth, who lost a toddler to a disease… something like that. It really puts whining or crying or whatever nonsense we're dealing with in perspective.

6. Sleep. Sometimes one of us will just go take a nap on a weekend afternoon.

5. Watch escapist TV. Or be part of it. Actually because we're part of it we hardly have time to watch it. Sometimes a delightfully bad movie hits the spot.

4. Drink heavily. Well, not heavily, just one. Bottle.

3. We share stories with other parents. Every single one of our friends has a worst-parent-in-the-world story. We are not alone.

2. Ask the boys to tell us a joke. Sometimes even if the kids are the ones stressing us out, they can snap us out of it, too! Johan slays us with his completely nonsensical knock-knock jokes, delivered with a perfectly straight face.

1. Remind ourselves that they grow up so fast, there will come a time when we're dying to have a little baby on our chests with a busy-body telling us everything we're doing wrong.

Chapter 9

If I Wouldn't Eat That, My Kid Won't Either

Dining In and Out

Alex

Baby food…mmmmmmm…not. Simon and I vowed when we had children that we would never feed them anything we weren't prepared to eat ourselves. I'm happy to say that we stuck to that: we never once gave either of them a jar of baby food or any type of unappetizing mush. They were exclusively nursed with (very) occasional formula supplement until six months, and then we started solids. We did not go nuts with introducing one food at a time every other day as some suggest. That seemed too much like hard work. As there were no allergies in our family anywhere, we decided to simply mash up a bit of whatever we were eating and see if the boys wanted to eat it. They both took to food like crazy, and for the most part devoured what we gave them. Some things that our kids loved around the six- to 12-month mark were mashed avocado, mild curries if we had the time or Simon's famous Dead Cow Sauce (Bolognese).

Simon

For many years I've been slow-cooking Bolognese sauce. I use ground sirloin, the best peeled Italian plum tomatoes, garlic, onion, preferably fresh basil and oregano, as well as lashings of Hungarian paprika before lastly adding tomato paste. When François came along and was old enough to watch us cook, I christened this Dead Cow Sauce, as I really wanted him to appreciate and understand what it is that we eat.

On many a shopping excursion to our local butcher, Los Paisanos, I've seen fellow customers raise their eyebrows as François and Johan would walk down the counter with me as they tried to identify what blob of cells came from which animal. As babies they'd both been read farmyard books and watched a few down on the farm DVDs, but neither of those sources prepared them for the fact that Angus the Bull gets slaughtered for our dining purposes. And while I wasn't about to explain the process with which they met their deaths, I certainly wanted them to realize that that lump of red meat was a piece of dead cow, or that shank with a little Australian flag on it was actually the humerus of a little lamb. One time as François and I were marching down the long counter identifying the dead cows, dead pigs, dead sheep, dead chickens and dead ducks this woman piped up and exclaimed, "What are you doing, trying to make him a vegetarian?" "No," I replied, I wanted to make them merely educated eaters, as I believe they should know as much about what they are eating, whether it be the animal it came from or whether their food is laden with high fructose corn syrup. In three of the four countries in which I have lived—Australia, the United Kingdom and now the United States of America—we've done our darnedest to make our food as non-threatening in the looks department as possible. I loved the year I spent living in Paris in the late '80s where I'd walk out onto the local shopping street to buy that night's dinner and the chicken, duck, pheasant and other game and they looked like birds! They had their feet and head still attached instead of some nicely sliced, skinned, packaged tray in the fridge at the local supermarket.

Alex

Simon and I are lucky that both sides of our families are pretty healthy. No one has diabetes, no one has weird allergies, most relatives don't even get the sniffles very often… "You can't kill us with an axe," intoned my Granny Lola, who lived to be 103. Even when we lived in the Midwest with all the fast-food temptations that existed, we always made a huge effort to eat natural foods and even grew our own where possible. I went to a Catholic elementary school run by high-tech hippie philosophers, and although the religion didn't stick, the idea of living off the land, being self-reliant and growing or making what you need came with me into adulthood. I also took on their fascination with computer technology, but that's another story. Fast-forwarding to the present day, I guess we'd call ourselves locavores. In our neighborhood in Brooklyn there are many farmer's markets, produce stands and grocery stores with nearby offerings. The families on our block all go in together to purchase a quarter cow or half a cow, and the meat arrives cut the way we specify. At a local cheese shop, they sell root vegetables from a farm in upstate New York, and if you really wanted to, and you'd have to be pretty bored to do so, you could log on to the farm's website and watch the harvest via webcam. The boys' school organizes fresh egg pickup, and milk pickup is available, too. I have threatened several times to buy a cow to keep in the backyard, but neither Simon nor our block association will let me do it.

I try to make as many things as I can from scratch, such as bread for sandwiches, yogurt, ice cream (to control the added sugar) and even ketchup. Particularly when I went back to work full-time, part of what made me feel better about being out of the house so much was knowing that I contributed as much as possible to their daily meals. We both love to cook—Simon is the master of stovetop stews, such as Coq au Vin or anything involving meat, mushrooms and olives. I'm the queen of baking and roasting, and once we finished our dream kitchen, our days of ordering in were basically over except for nights of bad planning and exhaustion.

When the boys were babies and young toddlers, dinnertime was easy. We pulled them up to the table in high chairs or booster seats and mashed up a small amount of whatever we were having, or if it was something we knew they wouldn't eat (chicken, for some reason), we'd scramble them an egg or make a peanut butter sandwich. Right, this is not a nut-free house. I recognize that there are homes out there where parents have to be vigilant about what comes in and keep EpiPens handy. I'm so very, very grateful that we don't have to do that.

At the age of about two, our fearless, eat-anything boys suddenly grew opinions. With that, their little mouths wired themselves shut. All at once, they wanted plain pasta or plain bread. Nothing else would do. Maybe plain fries. Definitely no vegetables, no meat, just plain pasta and a big glass of milk, please. Simon and I had counted many a time on feeding them Dead Cow Sauce, and suddenly even that was out of bounds. I hate to say it, but I remember being a very picky eater when I was a child, too. My seafood-loving family offered me oysters, shrimp and crayfish and I turned up my nose for years. They laughed, served me a piece of steak or a sandwich or whatever I wanted and moved on. At one point I started eating seafood and salads and other things again, and my mother said something to the effect of, "Yes, you've been missing out for years, but we knew you wouldn't starve and that meant more for the rest of us." And so it shall be with my children, I guess. François finally came through that phase and now happily eats Dead Cow Sauce, Australian meat pies and more. One sneaky thing we did during the pickiest time and still do with Johan, is to boil the plain pasta in chicken or beef stock so that at least a few nutrients soak into the carbohydrate extravaganza; Simon came up with that great idea. We have recently begun to make a little headway even with Johan toward normal eating, in that we can usually get them to try a bite of what's on our plate with the promise of dessert. We said we'd never bribe our children, but oh my yes, does the threat of no dessert work. Another thing we tried was to pick up a children's cookbook with lots of photos and have the boys go through and circle photos of the foods they'd like to try. After that exercise they ate salmon, zucchini and tacos. Once.

We've also tried getting them involved in cooking—something they both love. François excitedly signed up for a cooking elective after school and proudly brought home his creations—salad, a hamburger, pesto sauce, etc. In 10 weeks, the only one he ate was Monkey Bread. He's been asking to take the course again, promising that "this time I'll eat everything." Nowadays Johan repeatedly comes into the kitchen shouting, "I want to make a concoction!"

François and Johan Licking the Bowl

Concoction
by Johan van Kempen

Step 1: Retrieve big green bowl from cupboard and tap Mommy on the back with it. She'll get the idea.

Step 2: With help, assemble ingredients and measuring implements. Beg for eggs and ask Mommy whether any accidentally broke in the fridge and can be used for playtime.

Step 3: Add ½ c. flour, ½ c. sugar, 1 tsp salt, 1 or 2, maybe 3 tsps paprika (for the color) to bowl. Whisk violently—making sure to spill a little out of the top.

Step 4: Add something wet. Water will work, but make sure you ask Mommy for milk or melted butter. Depending on what she's doing she might say yes.

Step 5: Mix. Mix some more. Maybe a little more. Taste. Make a face and growl at the bowl menacingly. Taste again. Growling didn't make it taste any better.

Step 6: Ask Mommy for chocolate chips. If she gives you any, make sure to pull a couple out of the bowl to eat them.

Step 7: Pour the whole mess into a "Johan pan" (a particularly beloved cookie sheet) and put into the extra oven we only use once or twice a week.

Step 8: Laugh when Mommy remembers it's there, usually several days later.

Despite the struggles with picky eating, we always try to make family meals a time to eat and enjoy each other. Lately we always play I-Spy at the table, and François is really good at it. He'll stump us occasionally and often guess our obscure choices. Johan, however, keeps us guessing. He hasn't quite mastered yet that the thing he spies actually has to be in the room, so he'll say he spies something blue. After we've gone through everything blue within sight, he'll happily crow, "It's a blue whale, you lose!" For the record, there are no whales in our house or in Brooklyn that I know of. At least not real ones. We make sure that at the dinner table, napkins are in laps, cutlery is used and conversations are initiated. Some families we know draw topics out of a hat, but that seems a little forced to me. We're not quite at the point where we can require each child to bring a current event to discuss, but at least we can ask each boy what they did at school or the playground and play games.

When it comes to dining out, we like to chain our children to the table. One leg each, so it doesn't show. We lived through lots of teasing, admonition and holier-than-thou preaching after a particular episode of *Housewives* aired, one that showed François stabbing a kangaroo into the hamburger of a cast member at a dinner he should never have attended in a fancy restaurant that ran very late. Misbehavior to that extent really is rare for our kids, but it happens when the perfect storm of parental distraction, overtired children and too many people come together. Do take your children to good restaurants, just not at 10 p.m., so that they develop an appreciation for good food and grow up respecting dining establishments. If you only take your child to McDonalds or IHOP, they will grow up thinking that it's OK to run like a mad-man through restaurants, and that plastic, overprocessed food full of chemicals is acceptable. Particularly if given a chance to blow off steam before and after, children absolutely can learn to behave themselves in restaurants. Similar to our flight to Australia, I have to laugh when I see posts online of "sightings" of our family in restaurants. The discussion goes something like this:

> **TableHopper@RecognizedUs.com:** Saw Alex and Simon from RHONY last night. They seemed really low key and normal and their kids were very well behaved!
>
> **Incredulous@OnlySawTheFirstSeason.com:** No hamburgers were killed? Amazing.
>
> **ActualFriend@ThinksItsHilarious.com:** LOL, I know!

In urban areas diners are spoiled for choice. In our neighborhood alone there are 50-some establishments, most of which welcome or at least tolerate children. We learned a lot through experience, not the least of which is that in urban settings with so much competition, there are many great restaurants that welcome well-behaved children and manage to leave the adults with a feeling they've had a good meal without sacrificing themselves to big-box corporate chains or uninspiring food for the sakes of their offspring.

Our best bets are restaurants with plenty of things to see while waiting, such as fiery brick ovens, open kitchens where you can see the staff working, places with live music (Sunday brunches with bands are normally a hit) as well as almost any place with outdoor seating in good weather. Our neighborhood has a number of old-school French and Italian restaurants with gardens, most of which have pétanque or bocce courts where kids can stroll around between courses or even play a game with the old-timers.

We always bring distractions, such as a bag of books, small toys that are not small enough to get lost in someone's food, flash cards or coloring books. The flash cards with simple math are great, and sometimes even more entertaining than they are meant to be. We have a math deck with pictures of animals on it and recently Johan solemnly held up a card and said, "5 + 9 = Pigs." There were, in fact, pigs on the card, but not 14 of them. Another phase passed through involved drawing contests—the boys each draw as many pictures as they can before the food comes. Make quiet puppet theatre with forks if the restaurant is noisy. The bathroom can also be a fun place to visit when you're a little kid, particularly for the newly potty trained. In fact sometimes when we're out at a neighborhood restaurant where we know all the staff and most of the customers, we take a table close enough that they can walk in themselves.

This works well in familiar restaurants where we've been to the bathroom many times and only one person goes in at a time.

The biggest recipe for disaster with dining out is parental distraction. Like clockwork, every time Simon or I have had our attention pulled away from the kids at a meal in a restaurant, the boys get restless. It's as though they have an unspoken signal between the two of them, "Mom and Dad aren't looking. Quick! Into the kitchen to tackle the chef!" Ergo, we've learned the hard way to pay attention at all times. If someone's phone rings or someone comes up to the table to say hello, at least one of us concentrates on keeping the troops in their chairs.

TOP 10 THINGS WE DON'T LIKE ABOUT CHILDREN'S RESTAURANTS:

10.   The food is awful.

9.   Unruly behavior in children is tolerated more than in "grown-up" restaurants. Do you really want to be bitten in the leg by someone else's kid? Have they had a rabies shot?

8.   Parents get annoyed by #10 and #9 and don't watch their children closely. Those kids spin out of control and tempt your kids into misbehaving.

---

7. Mayhem ensues.

6. You lose your child. François convinced us to have a birthday party at Chuck E. Cheese, and when the dancing mouse came out to put on the happy birthday show, we couldn't find him as he'd disappeared into the crawling maze.

5. Our kids won't eat any of the cutesy items on the menu anyway.

4. I'd rather talk to my kids about the interesting paintings on the wall instead of whatever Cartoon Network is playing above their heads.

3. Servers for some reason tend pay more attention to kids when they're the only ones in a restaurant as opposed to one of a hundred.

2. Adult restaurants have a better wine selection.

1. Where would you rather be? A bistro devoted to race-car driving, with 1950s toy cars on the walls, or T.G.I. Friday's?

Chapter 10

You'll Give in Before I Do!

The Art and Warfare of Bedtime

In 2008 we went through a gut renovation of our home and the boys had to share a room for over a month. For the most part they enjoyed being close, but at times they got on each other's nerves.

Johan:	I want to go up.
Alex:	Where?
Johan:	To the top bunk
François:	No, I'm on the top bunk
Johan:	I WANT THE TOP BUNK!
François:	NO, I WAS HERE FIRST!
Alex:	Johan, would you like to sleep with Mommy and Daddy?
Johan & François:	YES!

```
(continued)
Alex:        Four of us won't fit. François, you slept
             with us last night so it's Johan's turn.
François:    (Screaming) You hate me!
Alex:        Actually I love you. How about you
             sleep on the bottom bunk—that way
             I can snuggle with you for a few min-
             utes now, plus you'll be close to the
             ground and can run into our room if
             you wake up early.
François:    OK.
Alex:        So, Johan, you may have the top
             bunk.
Johan:       Yippee!!
```

As our boys have grown they've continued to sleep well and we know we're fortunate—I've heard horror stories about kids who don't sleep. From birth we were very laissez-faire about sleeping/crying, and sort of followed our instincts with a little validation from Dr. Michel Cohen (*The New Basics*). The end result? Two healthy sleepers who, after the negotiation of who is sleeping where, what PJs are worn, which stories are read, in which order and language, drop off pretty quickly once the lights are off.

Once the boys moved into portable cribs, we started putting them down with a bottle of water. Having heard cautionary tales about tooth decay, I can count on one hand the times the boys fell asleep with anything other than water in the bottle, and that was always by accident. Both kids grew to reach up their hands for the water bottle, and even years later at four and six they have squeeze bottles of water available at their bedsides. We did briefly take them away when transitioning between nighttime pull-up diapers and no diapers, but as soon as they mastered getting up to use the potty, we returned the water.

Simon
Negotiating with children is the art of (sometimes) letting them feel that they've gained a concession while unbeknownst to them having them end up at the same place. As soon as François could both express himself and use reason, I became a great proponent in using reverse psychology. Now, as he gets older, he's more and more seeing through said psychology. Fortunately he's not querying it for Johan and so I reckon I've another 18 plus months to continue it on him.

François: I don't want to go to bed yet, Daddy.
Simon: Oh, that's fine. You don't need sleep. The rats, the ghosts and the ghouls told me they wanted your company tonight. Where shall I tell them you'll meet them?
François: Dad, I'm feeling tired.
Simon: 'Night, son!

Alex

This is not to say that getting to the lights out part every evening is easy... far from it. Our biggest challenge is winding the boys down at night—we typically "come home" at 6:15 p.m., Simon from his office and me from either the home office or various meetings, and they are ecstatic to see us and bounding around like adorably hyperactive puppies. The next hour is a race to get dinner on the table for them and us, and then into the bedtime hour to have them asleep between 8 and 8:30 p.m. They never want to start reading stories because they know it means bedtime is nigh, and once we start reading they never want to stop because they love it (actually, so do we). We found it's best to keep an eye on the clock and start moving them toward their room(s) about 15 minutes before we want to start reading, giving 10- and five-minute warnings until "get in your room" time. I wish I could say we're wildly successful at this, but mostly we're not. It's always a struggle to get all four family members to sit down to dinner in time to be finished by 7:30 p.m. Simon typically walks in the door still working from his BlackBerry, and likes to sit down and relax before eating. My time is divided between making dinner for the family quickly enough that no one goes around looking for snacks. Snacks and TV are the death knell for an on-time lights-out. Snacks spoil dinner and if the TV goes on, parents start talking to one another and debriefing the day, and dinner gets pushed back another half hour. Why is this important? The kids get very cranky if they are rushed through bedtime. It's important and valuable to have 40 minutes of conversation and stories read as well as teeth brushing and dragon-slaying. Slaying the dragon is our family euphemism for using the toilet (drowning the dragons that live in the sewer) and is fun for the boys to talk about, though probably not forever. Hmm, perhaps I should delete this—I don't want obnoxious classmates getting hold of this book in 10 years and asking the boys if they need to slay the dragon in the middle of geometry class. On nights that we find ourselves stuck between canceling story and talk time or getting the boys to bed late, we always get tears and tantrums in lieu of stories, so we do our best to start the bedtime routine as early as possible.

Although we try to calm them down over two hours, sometimes we'll get to 8 p.m. and they're still on speed. Five books later, François might be asleep while Johan is bouncing up and down on his bed and singing at the top of his lungs. At that point we normally remove Johan from the room and let him wind down a little, then try again. We've also occasionally succumbed to our own exhaustion and simply lay down to sleep ourselves. Whoever is still awake normally climbs into our bed after he sees us going to sleep. Now that François can read on his own, he wants to read to us before bed versus being read to. Johan has little patience for François' pace and level of reading and would rather have us read him something more advanced than watch François read—with this we either split up the reading duties or stagger bedtime. The former works better than the latter!

It is getting a little easier as they get older. I remember lying on François' bed for nearly an hour at night before Johan was born, and that could get painful, both emotionally and physically. We also had to police naps, and make sure that no sleeping happened after 2 p.m. or else we knew they'd be up until 10 p.m. Now they are both old enough to know they need sleep, which is something, at least. When they do get overtired and cranky, I always remind them that they are cranky because they're tired. Recently I was exhausted and snapped at the boys for something relatively minor. François said, "Mommy, can you go to bed when we do tonight? You're cranky and you need your sleep." Out of the mouths of babes...

One of the most frustrating things about bedtime is that the boys invariably turn into great conversationalists as the lights go out. Each night when I give them a quick snuggle before leaving the room, I get questions such as, "What should I do if someone calls another kid 'stupid' at school?" or "How do I stop throwing tantrums?" These are things I wish they would ask long before bedtime, and it's simultaneously a delaying tactic and a really interesting discussion.

Alex:	Good night, François. (Begins to leave the room.)
François:	Wait!! I have a problem!
Alex:	What's that, kiddo?
François:	There's going to be a battle on my bed!
Alex:	(Suspicious.) Why?
François:	There's an orca and a dolphin on my bed, and orcas eat dolphins. (I glance over and amidst the 15 or so stuffed toys on the bed there is indeed a dolphin and a killer whale.)
Alex:	How about I take one of them with me?
François:	I don't know if I can sleep then!
Alex:	(Thinking fast.) Just tell the orca that he's a dolphin, too, and cannibalism isn't allowed in our house.
François:	GREAT idea, Mom—good night!

Bedtime away from home often winds up being easier for us—maybe it's the excitement of a new bed. Everywhere we go, we take sharks and squishies. François has a plush hammerhead shark puppet and Johan a great white shark. They also each have a small lavender pillow tied in a bow that they call their "squishies," presumably because they are, in fact, squishy. With those two implements, the boys are usually willing to be tucked into whatever bed is available as long as they know we're nearby. The only time we get into trouble is when we're in connecting rooms in a hotel. If there are two phone lines, the boys love to call one another. This is all fine and dandy until they wind up accidentally calling the front desk, room service or the business center.

We also have a few things we say to each other as we leave the room—we always say, "Good night, I love you, see you in the morning," in both English and French. Also, for some reason we've been saying, "No monsters, no masks, no flippers, no ghosts," with a response of "Yay!" for years. I have no real recollection of how this got started—it may have been by one of our au pairs, but in any case both boys and parents think it's cute, so we always say it as we're leaving the room and closing the door behind us.

Alex: Goodnight, Johan. I love you.
Johan: I love the Grinch.
Alex: Oh. OK then. (Walks to the doorway.)
Johan: (singing out from his bed) And you, too, Mommy!
Alex: Thanks, kid.

Simon
All through my life I have never had an issue with falling or staying asleep—sorry, drug companies, but you'll be

getting no sleeping pill business from me. But where this has been a hindrance is when each boy was between two and three years old and required one of us to lie down with them after the bedtime routine to get them off to sleep. When this routine follows (and it usually does) an evening when the four of us have eaten dinner together, then more often than not I'll fall asleep, too. Once asleep Alex knows it's practically pointless trying to awaken me and so more often than not on nights like this I'll sleep for three or four hours, squeezed into a twin size bed next to Johan. Eventually I awaken and stumble into my own bed. Invariably sometime through the next day I'll realize I have a stiff neck, stiff back and resolve to not fall asleep with them, but to make it to my own bed before so doing.

Alex

So the cute little monsters are safely tucked into bed and we've tiptoed or negotiated out of the room. Now comes the fun in the middle of the night. No, I'm not talking about fun for Simon and me (see chapter five), but those moments when we are wakened from a deep sleep, or rather I am, as Simon sleeps like a corpse, to hear a screaming child. We only dealt with nightmares once or twice—a real anomaly for us—but we do sometimes get boys who have to hit the bathroom. I'll never forget one night when François was just getting through nighttime toilet training. We had a potty next to the bed so that he could just roll out and take care of business. At the time we still used the baby monitor, and we smiled at each other in parental pride as we heard him get up, fumble around, urinate and get back into bed. A few minutes later I went to the bathroom myself and discovered that his bedroom potty was NOT in his room because it was in the bathtub full of disinfectant. The next morning, there was a wet spot on the floor next to his bed where the potty should have been. Oops. From then on, checking potty placement was added to the nightly checklist.

Sleepy Johan After a Nap

If the nighttime sleeps have been relatively painless for us, daytime naps have always been a different story. Here our kids are different: Johan loves his afternoon nap, and even at three and a half still liked a short one after lunch. François, on the other hand, *never* wants to go to sleep in the afternoon. At about age one and a half, we started having to wheel him around in the stroller to get him to sleep. It wound up being the only way, and I would structure my day around the noontime walk. If we didn't get him to sleep between 12–2 p.m. or 1–3 p.m., he'd basically fall asleep standing up at about 4:30–5 p.m. and then would never want to go to bed at night. Not fun, particularly when I was freelancing and planned to do design work and take phone calls during those precious two hours. That's one element of early childhood I was not sorry to leave behind. I also hated having to check up on our au pair with the naps when they were on duty. We discovered that it was very tempting for our 18- or 20-year-old au pairs to give up the fight at midday and just allow François to fall asleep later on. It was then our problem, not theirs, when we came home and had to put them to bed. During our weekly check-in meetings we often had to tell our au pair to stop letting him fall asleep so late, and one year it wound up being a three-way battle when I ultimately laid down the law. Funnily enough F-Bomb has become an ally in keeping his little brother awake. He's learned that Johan falling asleep in the late afternoon is bad news, and thinks nothing of shrieking in J-Boy's ear, pulling him off the couch and chanting, "Don't fall asleep or I'll eat you," and generally making it impossible to doze off. Johan usually either starts pounding him or joins in the raucousness.

TOP 20 BEDTIME STORIES:

20. *Asterix the Gaul* by Albert Uderzo

19. *The Man Who Walked Between the Towers* by Mordecai Gerstein

18. *Et Si Le Loup y'Etait* by Maïté Laboudigue

17. *Le Monde Merveilleux des mes Trois Ans* by Sophie Maraval-Hutin

16. *The Very Silly Shark* by Jack Tickle

15. *Aussie Jingle Bells* by Colin Buchanan

14. *Chien de Lune* by David Spence

13. *I Live in Brooklyn* by Mari Takabayashi

12. *Hattie and the Fox* by Mem Fox

11. *One Small Place by the Sea* by Barbara Brenner

10. *Hairy Maclary from Donaldson's Dairy* by Lynley Dodd

9. *The Terrible Underpants* by Kaz Cooke

8. *In the Night Kitchen* by Maurice Sendak

7. All the poetry from *Where the Sidewalk Ends* by Shel Silverstein

6. *The Icky, Sticky Frog* by Dawn Bentley

5. *Frog and Toad are Friends* by Arnold Lobel

4. *The Australian Twelve Days of Christmas* by Heath Mackenzie

3. *Dr. Dog* by Babette Cole

2. *The Magic School Bus* Series by Joanna Cole

1. *Mike Mulligan and His Steam Shovel* by Virginia Lee Burton

TOP 10 LULLABIES:

10. "Mack The Knife" by Three Penny Opera

9. "Hit The Road, Jack" by Percy Mayfield/Ray Charles

8. "Imagine" by John Lennon

7. "All That Jazz" from Chicago

6. "Goodnight, My Someone" from *The Music Man*

5. "People Will Say We're In Love" by Oklahoma

4. "The Ballad of Jenny" by Three Penny Opera

3. Brahm's "Lullaby" with made-up lyrics by Alex

2. "Tomorrow" from *Annie*

1. "When You're Good To Mama" from *Chicago*

Chapter 11

Children Like Shiny Objects

Adventures with Valuables and Other Household Knick-Knacks

Just about every new parent has had a knee-jerk reaction where they want to remove anything that could possibly harm their child, or that their child could destroy, from the home. This includes (but is not limited to) anything poisonous, dangerous or breakable. No tchotchkes, nothing small enough to fit in their mouths, nothing they could tear apart. Nothing messy, nothing spilly, nothing trashy, nothing silly. In short, live in an empty house with no windows. Childproofing begins with keeping children safe from danger within the house, but it doesn't stop there. Unless parents decide to pad the floors and walls, remove anything remotely nice from the home, sit and sleep on the floor to prevent falls and only eat with spoons, childproofing also includes teaching your children how to respect furniture and valuables and to learn to live in a grown-up (albeit kid-friendly) environment.

Alex

By the time François was one we were getting itchy feet. Not about the Big City or our favorite part, Brooklyn—we loved the borough and couldn't imagine leaving. It was our apartment. Between the annoying neighbors and the increasing feeling that the neighborhood, Park Slope, was turning from a laid-back naturalist preserve to an increasingly dogmatic commune, we felt there might be something better just around the corner. When we bought an apartment two years previously, we both knew it was a starter apartment and wouldn't stay long. With one baby and plans for another, we began thinking that just a terrace didn't cut it—with kids we needed a yard. The point was driven home one afternoon when one of our cats chased a squirrel off the terrace and fell to her death (which occurred 10 hours after we'd run up a $2,000 vet bill frantically trying to save her life). François was beginning to walk, and I'd just discovered I was pregnant with Johan. In 2005 the real estate market was hot, hot, hot and we'd recently completed a gut renovation with all the bells and whistles every apartment-hunting couple in the city demanded. We were very lucky to a) find a couple willing to pay more than double our original purchase price for the triplex, and b) find a townhouse in an even better neighborhood in Brooklyn with a garden and a grassy yard for the right price. The day we moved in, not-quite-two-year-old François spent an hour running from the front of the house, out the back door and to the end of the yard. He was amazed, and we were proud to have solved our concrete jungle issue. Now, at 6:30 a.m. when the boys are up on a Saturday or when they want to spend "just five minutes" making snow angels, we can open the back door and let them at it, and instead of spending half an hour packing up a bag with extra mittens and making sure they have all the pieces of their snowsuits together, I can have them throw boots and a coat on over their PJs, and five minutes later throw two soaking wet, happy boys into a hot bath.

The townhouse we bought had great "bones" and original detail but needed renovation. We love to gut places and create spaces we relish, and began making plans to do the same with our new house. Over a period of about 22 months we dug our basement down two feet, underpinned the foundation, removed the back wall of the house on two floors, and finally did the cosmetics as well.

Prior to the renovation, we let quite a few things slide because we knew we'd be tearing out interiors and we had two little boys who spilled things and broke things and tripped while carrying markers. When our family was photographed at home for *New York* magazine, I didn't even notice that there was crayon on the wall until I saw the published picture. Knowing that the floors were going to be ripped up anyway, I was less inclined to be alarmed when I saw Johan prying up pieces of floorboard in the corner. With two boys at varying degrees of toilet training, we mopped the floors often and didn't worry much about what got deposited on them. If François wanted to pick up a miniature hammer and help Daddy smash a plaster façade that someone had tastelessly put up over the fireplace that was fine with me. Although it wasn't the only reason, we did have it in the backs of our minds that the longer we took with our renovation, the less likely we'd be to have boys who couldn't understand that it wasn't OK to draw on the walls and lick the furniture. Well, we're still working on the licking. Luckily, by the time we finished our home renovation, both boys were well out of diapers and past the handprints on the wall phase. They do like to stand on one kitchen counter and try to fly to the other, but I think I was still doing that at age eight or nine, so there's no point in trying to thwart genetics.

Partners in Crime

During the work we packed up everything in the house we didn't use often, and while doing so, I put all my jewelry in a lock box for safekeeping. Now, we're not billionaires and I don't own the Hope Diamond, but I am lucky enough to own several beautiful pieces that are more than a little valuable. We didn't want to move out of the house completely—we'd done that while gutting our previous apartment and felt it was a mistake, so we created a "green zone" within the house that we lived in while construction went on around us. As we moved our green zone around the house, we moved the jewelry lock box as well. While tidying up on a Sunday afternoon, I noticed that one pair of earrings and a necklace were missing. They were not a matching set, and I had just recently worn each of them to different events. I felt sure that I would have noticed if they had been gone long. I tried to retrace my steps after each event and remembered putting them away on both occasions. Where, then, could they be? Over the next three days I became more anxious as I checked all the various places besides the jewelry drawer where they might have been left. Makeup kit, no. Interior pockets of each purse I'd carried in the last week, no. On Thursday, just as I was trying to remember whether these pieces had been added to our policy the last time I updated our insurance, I opened the lock box to get out another pair of earrings, and was very surprised to find the missing pieces safe in the box. A little voice behind me asked, "Is that the right place for them, Mommy?" I whirled around to find François smiling at me hopefully. I asked what he meant. "On Sunday when you were packing, I took those out. I put them in my pocket and when I was done, I put them back." My dear son carried several thousand dollars worth of jewelry around in his jeans pocket for a day or two including to school and back, then thoughtfully returned them?!? I have no idea why he wanted them or what he did with them other than carrying them around, but they appeared unscathed. This presented a quandary. On the one hand, I was pitifully grateful that he'd brought them back. On the other, he should never have taken them out to begin with. I carefully explained this to him, and we forged a deal that he would be allowed to hold or try on my jewelry, but only with me supervising. I can live with that.

Keys, Jewelry, It All Tastes Good

It's not just shiny objects but gooey ones, too, that attract little fingers. While writing a business proposal one afternoon, François and Johan ran up behind me. "What kind of toothpaste is this, Mommy?" I turned around and there they were, brandishing a positively ancient tube of, ahem, personal lubricant. Assessing the damage, I asked, "You didn't brush your teeth with it, did you?" "No, we wanted to find out what flavor it was first." Whew. "That's not toothpaste, guys." "What is it, Mommy?" Thinking fast, I said, "It's lubricant. You use it to get yourself unstuck, say if you got your hand or your head stuck in a fence." We had just read a funny story about a girl who threw a tantrum and stuck her head in a fence—her rescue involved a neighbor putting butter on her neck—so I thought they might understand. "OK, we understand you, Mommy," said François. Now, of course I've set myself up to hear the words, "Mom, I'm stuck! Get the KY!!" Luckily it hasn't happened yet. They are probably waiting for our next cocktail party.

Our boys also love shoes. This is not particularly profound information, as both Mommy and Daddy share this obsession. I have a few precious pairs of sandals with fun things like crystals, gold roping, seashells and beads on them, which are tantalizing and tempting to young boys. After a few attempts at wearing my heels, they realized there was not much fun in walking like grown-up girls and did other things like use them as puppets. I have to say, in the garden when we're having a cocktail at 6 p.m., it's kind of fun to watch their Roberto Cavalli puppet theatre with a seashell mermaid battling a crystal leafy tree against a backdrop of the setting sun.

Simon

Not long after François was born I remember visiting a children's store in the Hasidic section of Crown Heights to use a gift certificate we'd been given by a friend who lived in the area. We'd already accumulated all the things we thought we'd need for our new little baby so at this store we decided to buy things we'd need later on, or so we thought. And so it was in late 2003 we bought a wooden gate to be affixed at the top of stairs. It went unused and was still in its box until we sold it via a parents' Listserv in 2008. And that toddler gate just about sums up my view about childproofing our home—we didn't. Yes, at about 14 months old while descending the stairs, François tumbled down the last four or so, but he learned that he needed to be careful on stairs and has never fallen again. While François has been to ER for stitches on two occasions, out of our visits there, neither boy has ever had an accident in the home that required medical attention. Have we been lucky? Sure, but we also have always striven to ensure that our boys understood the dangers around them.

Alex

The main rule we employ is that the children are allowed to touch things as long as they are gentle and we supervise. We've tried to instill in them a respect for valuables and nice environments. After completing our living room and dining room renovation, the boys were in awe of the finished product for a little while. They quickly made themselves at home and could see the difference between the previous mess and the current well-put-together rooms. Consequently, it really hasn't been difficult at all to get them to keep their food and drink on the table and off the sofas, to take off their shoes before jumping on chairs and to enter the house downstairs through the mud room if they're muddy, soggy or sticky. They wash their hands when they come into the kitchen, knowing that I'll let them "help" me if they do. They appreciate and respect valuables, though the tradeoff has been that they constantly lose game pieces. If it comes down to it, I'd rather lose checkers than cufflinks. One kind of funny thing I noticed recently is that the toys the boys tend to leave upstairs in our red and black living room often tend to be red and black as well. I'm not sure whether that's intentional, but it's funny that the room always seems to match regardless of its contents. They've also amassed a few valuable things themselves—last summer they picked up some beautiful seashells when visiting friends in the Hamptons. Both François and Johan carefully keep the shells in baskets and handled them with more care than I've ever seen them use with their other treasures.

I know there will be hiccups along the way. There will be broken glasses, gouged floorboards, chipped tiles and yanked strings. I remember being much older than they are now and shinnying up a doorway, crouched ready to drop down onto the unsuspecting shoulders of my brother or mother's friends. There were so many crazy things I used to do, including tying my Barbie dolls to misappropriated yarn and rappelling them up and down the freshly polished wooden staircase. One time I proudly tried on my brand-new puffy snow parka and leaned against the glass doors of a friend's fireplace, only to discover that the back of the parka melted and left a gaping hole in the coat and a sticky, impossible to clean mess on the fireplace door.

When we leave the house, New York City surrounds us and it's very different than the places Simon and I grew up. When I was six there were no taxis to avoid when crossing the street, no bicyclists careening across a bridge and nearly hitting me, no tourists walking five abreast on a city sidewalk. In the city the kids ride on our shoulders quite a bit more than we ever did with our parents, in order to see above the crowds on Fifth Avenue during the holidays. At their age I barely registered that there were other cars on the road, much less commented on other people's driving skills. The other day someone cut Simon off on the Brooklyn Bridge and as he swore, François piped up, "That's a bad word, Daddy, but it's OK because he was a really stupid driver," which reminds me that eventually we're going to have to teach them to drive. Maybe we'll do that in Australia—I can't imagine being able to make the mistakes I did learning to drive in Kansas, on Atlantic Avenue in Brooklyn. Ultimately our philosophy of childproofing comes down to this—we try to keep them safe whenever we can. We teach them to respect their surroundings and objects and after that, we don't cry over spilled milk or Chardonnay.

TOP 10 CRAZIEST PLACES WE'VE FOUND OBJECTS:

10. Remote control car key, one piece found in a child's rain boot in his closet, the other piece wedged in the radiator.

9. Valid American Express card, in François' underwear drawer.

8. Batteries, in the cat food jar.

7. Plastic taxicab, found in a puddle on the bottom of the oven after I preheated it to 500 degrees to make pizza.

6. Magic marker on a painting, where somebody (I still don't know who) added a tail to a previously tailless dog.

5. Unused monthly subway pass, worth about $90, in a toy cash register in the playroom.

4, Important business cards from networking meetings, found in washing machine after going through a cycle in a kid's jeans pocket.

---

3.   Cat's toothbrush, carefully placed in the family toothbrush holder in the master bathroom. We replaced all human ones after that discovery.

2.   Used nighttime transition diapers, in the laundry basket.

1.   Simon's best watch... missing for the last four months. If you come over and happen to see it, will you let us know?

Chapter 12

Raising Baby Einsteins

The Race to Offer Your Children Every Advantage

Baby videos really are addictive. No way do they make your two-month-old smarter, despite the spin on the packaging. Though apparently some parents really believed that and consequently got their money back. The videos certainly do help stressed out parents relax and keep themselves from stamping the baby's forehead "return to sender." At some point in your sleep-deprived stage you'll find a screaming or wide-awake infant at 3:30 in the morning or some ungodly hour, and put on one of those classical music baby DVDs. We absolutely double-dog dare you not to be completely transfixed by the calming waves set to Handel's *Water Music*. We firmly believe that they are as soothing for the frazzled new parent as they are for the child. When you're so exhausted that you begin to wonder who you are, and if it would be OK to just cry along with the baby, pop in a video. Pour yourself a gin as well if you think that will help. You will slowly be transported into a happy place, even more so if it's four o'clock in the morning. Just be sure to not drop the baby. Where's that vibrating bouncy chair?

Alex

After François was born I found myself kind of annoyed by people who preach "tummy time," and make weird faces to babies. I also thought that the whole teaching-babies-sign-language thing had to be a scheme dreamed up by ASL experts who wanted to sell classes to easily influenced new parents. Babies may be able to make a sign with their hands, but what are they going to tell you other than, "I'm happy, I'm sad, change my diaper, I'm hungry"? I'm not convinced they have the emotional maturity to choose which sign to make, and I'd rather figure it out myself by process of elimination rather than trying to teach a pig to fly—not that I think my kids can fly…

There's a product out there for every type of neurosis a first-time parent might have, whether it's sign language, baby videos or stupid Velcro thingies that are supposed to help you swaddle a baby. Incidentally, our boys hated being swaddled and would squirm, kick and carry on until they were free. They loved the really loose sleep sacks, but swaddling? "No, thank you, Mommy!" "Uh-uh, Daddy! Leave me alone!" Living in the city, where there tend to be a lot of neurotic people anyway, there are many parents who fill up their narrow townhouses or tiny apartments with every bloody thing they can buy, hoping that they'll find the one magic product that turns their child into the best student in preschool, or just keeps them from screaming through the night. We were no better at this than anyone else— there are loads of things (like swaddlers, diaper pad covers, pacifier holders) we bought with François that we never used. We also got sucked into the talking toy madness. You know the educational ones where you push a button or turn a page and they talk to you? We get annoyed by them, but kids love them, and if you throw them across the room in frustration, they are big and heavy enough to break something (so you can't do that). One thing we did to ease the pain was to insist that if a talking toy came into our house, it had to speak a foreign language or speak English in an accent other than American. Consequently we speak to our irritating toys in French, Italian or Spanish: "Jouet avec moi!" "Buona Sera, Ragazzi!" "Hola, mis amigos!" My personal favorite is the British farm animal toy that features a male voice (think Hugh Grant) deadpanning, "I'm a cow. I eat grass." That one is kind of fun to listen to after the children are in bed and we've had a few glasses of cham- pagne. There's also a phone with colored shapes that says, "Red Circle," but the overly chipper Mary Poppins-ish voice sounds like she's saying, "Red Psycho." Even Johan thinks so. These days François likes to sneak up behind people and turn on the Italian one so that it abruptly starts counting, "Uno, due, tre," and then run away giggling.

Sometimes after Johan was born I'd wheel him to the park and let him sleep while François played. I would over- hear mothers talking about gross motor skill development, which of course is important, but do we need to obsessively monitor every developmental move of our children? Can he pick up a piece of pasta and shove it in his ear? Great, his manual skills are on track. Can he express himself clearly enough to scream, "Mommy, wipe my bottom!" and do I understand him? Fantastic, his speech is as it should be. Is Johan able to snatch toys away from his big brother and land a punch on his nose without missing? Perfect aim—these boys are going to develop beautifully. There are moms I know who test their children constantly and rely on outside opinions to tell them what to do to make their kids stronger, faster and better. Do I want my kids to fall behind? Of course not! Do I think that they may well learn better and faster by my playing creative games with them rather than sitting them down and cramming for standardized tests? Yes.

Simon

As someone who loved learning more when not in a super structured environment, I started challenging François and then Johan to be aware of what is around them by incorporating the things we saw into seemingly innocuous questions. Often when walking with them I would ask them to find patterns in things, to identify numbers and letters on building signs and so forth. Also my 10 fingers get a constant workout, as I am always using them to teach simple addition, subtraction, multiplication and division— of course with never actually using those terms. After doing this for a little while I no longer have to prod either of them to look around them, as they just seemed to start pointing out to me the shapes, letters and numbers that they saw, and even the differences in accents between Alex and me.

Simon:	What's that street sign say?
François:	Court Street.
Simon:	How is your age similar to the number of letters in the street's name?
François:	(Thinks for a minute.) Oh, I am five and "C-o-u-r-t" has five letters in it!
Johan:	Daddy, is that like "one, two, three, four, five, once I caught a fish alive"?
Simon:	(Laughing) Only in England or Australia —Mommy doesn't say it that way. Court and caught are antonyms.
Johan:	Huh? Is that like bugs?
Simon:	Nevermind—we'll get to that later.

Alex

Let's talk about Mommy and Me classes. I think they're a good idea, but not really for teaching anything. I think parents should absolutely sign up for a music class at six months so that you and your baby have somewhere to go and meet other babies and moms. Did François or Johan participate and clap along to the music? Nope. Absolutely not at that age. It turns out that Johan was more interested in music classes than his older brother, and he caught on by about 18 months. François, on the other hand, didn't take to music much but in art class would spend the entire period painting one masterpiece. Fair enough. When they were babies they both liked to try and shove all the musical instruments into their mouths. Teachers are usually prepared for this and have a supply of wipes on hand—when you finally pry the shaky eggs from your drooling baby's mouth, give them a wipe and you're good to go. These classes are fun for moms to socialize and secretly make fun of other people's children, but that's about it. I'm glad I started early so that I had something to do, and once they were old enough to participate more fully, I knew all the teachers and had a better idea of what they would really like. After a few years of going to the same wonderful studio, we worked out that Johan likes music with English- or French-speaking teachers, and François likes art or physically active classes in English only—for French he prefers a class purely about learning the language. Along the way we made lots of friends and both their caregivers and I had fun. Everyone wins!

Sleeplessness is a recurring theme throughout parenthood and it rears its ugly head again a few years later. Once you get past the baby phase and blast through the motor skill development phase, the chanting in Arabic phase (OK, I made that one up), you eventually get to the "applying to school phase," which is where all urban parents turn into wailing, nocturnal, type-A obsessed harridans willing to sleep with persons not their spouse if they think it will help their child get into THE RIGHT SCHOOL. Although

we resisted stressing out too much, we endured this process as well. I am absolutely beyond elated that Johan was
accepted to the pre-K program at François' elementary
school. No, this was not a private school where interviews,
application fees and recommendations changed hands in
hopes of being awarded the privilege of paying $30,000
per year per child for a junior kindergarten program. The
finger-drumming, obsessive refreshing of the "check e-mail"
button and backup-plan plotting was over a spot in a public
school. People think New Yorkers and other urban dwellers
are crazy. Trust me, we're not.

We bought our townhouse in the zone of one of the
best elementary school districts in the city, which I'll call
PS Fabulous. We knew how difficult the private school
application process was, particularly for parents like us
with no family connections to any particular school. We
wanted to be sure that if we were unable to place our boys
in private school right away, that they would have a great
public school alternative. Aren't we so smart and prepared?
Ha! It turns out that there are so many hundreds of children in our school zone, which is only a few square blocks,
that a lottery is necessary for those valuable 54 places in
pre-K. Our first year after François had been wait-listed at
both the private schools to which we'd applied, we entered
the pre-K lottery at PS Fab. François' name was drawn
at number 10 on the wait list, which at the time may as
well have been number 650. He hadn't gotten in, and we
were crushed. It had nothing to do with his abilities or test
scores, but just the luck of the draw. Simon attended the

drawing and phoned me immediately at the office once he'd found out. In anticipation of the F-Bomb being wait-listed, I was standing by from work with a spreadsheet of nearby schools with pre-K programs, and the phone number of our zone's district office within the Board of Education. After a quick call, I narrowed down the list to schools without lotteries and that brought the list down to one. Only one school was kinda sorta within walking distance, had a pre-K program and no lottery. It was near a housing project, and was an integration school where students with high-functioning disabilities were mixed with the class. We decided on both counts that it would bring diversity to the classroom, and in the case of the latter, help teach François tolerance at a young age. It wasn't a done deal; I called "PS Just OK" and they said that parents were already calling for spots. I convinced them to hold onto one for François since we'd called before any parents who might walk in later that day, and promised that Simon or I would walk his file over to the school within 24 hours.

After moving into the neighborhood specifically for PS Fab, we were heartbroken and angry that we couldn't get in and had to take François further away to PS Just OK in the next zone. Far from the urban flight of the past few decades, people haven't been moving to the suburbs once kid number one or even number two comes along. They, like us, admit their addiction to the urban environment. Does needing to live within one block of an all-night oyster bar mean you have to sacrifice your kids' education? That's where the "Me" generation morphs into the "We" (no, not the Wii—we haven't gotten there yet). We couldn't believe that there were so many kids in a few square blocks that our neighborhood school couldn't take them all, and the school we were able to enroll François in was only four long blocks away but might as well have been on Mars in terms of the composition. In Brooklyn we say "long blocks and short blocks" like Manhattanites say "avenue blocks and street blocks."

As the last few years of our lives have been well-documented thanks to our reality show experience, sometimes time lines get blurred and viewers think that something which happened six months or a year ago happened yesterday. Predictably, this happened with something very close to our hearts—school enrollment. We went through the drama of PS Fab versus PS OK while we filmed season one of *Housewives*. Simon was angry and frustrated the day he spoke on camera about our son only getting into what he sarcastically called our 14th choice school. A couple of weeks later we nearly started levitating in excitement when we received a call that a seat had opened up at PS Fab, and immediately switched François over. The following year when the show aired, some parents watched and thought that we were insulting PS Fab, which we weren't. A quick conversation with the principal, his teacher and the class parents cleared that up, and we happily settled into the rhythm of his new school. Two years later, we went through the same nerve-racking process to place Johan at PS Fab. Although there is an enrolled family priority policy, there was a question as to whether there would be more than 54 siblings applying to pre-K. I know—it's crazy. The fact that there are potentially 54 four-year-olds with older brothers and sisters in one particular school, all in a few short blocks, is kind of mind-blowing. That's New York, my friends.

Simon

Since mid-2005 (before François' second birthday), Alex and I started on the hunt for the right school for him. When we'd moved to Park Slope, Brooklyn from the Upper West Side of Manhattan in 2001, despite not having children at that time, we had ensured that we bought a co-op in one of the best elementary school zones in Brooklyn: PS321. At that stage the choice was as much for maintaining good property values than anything else. When we decided that our three-bedroom co-op was going to be too small for a family of four about to take on a live-in au pair and started our new house search, at the top of our list was to be within a great school zone. Yes, we wanted to go the private route, but perhaps it's my caution gained from losing my father at such a young age, that I know too well how quickly life can change. It is always best to be as prepared as possible. One thing I wasn't prepared for was the very young age that schooling can start these days. I remember my mother being very proud that I was allowed to start school at four years, nine months, and how my then early admission was only down to the fact that a few months earlier I'd beaten the headmaster's 12-year-old son at poker. But there's a huge difference from being almost five and going off to school than with François, who started a three-days a week program before his third birthday and five full days of school before his fourth. Likewise, Johan started four days a week before his third birthday and in the fall of 2009 joined his big brother at a full five days a week of schooling.

Johan Graduates Preschool!

Yes, I know there are those that say that schooling for two-, three- and even four-year-olds is just expensive day care and the best children can benefit is learning some sharing skills and dealing with peers. Until this experience I would have been fairly sympathetic to that viewpoint. But having watched the development of my sons, attended Parent-Teacher Nights to discuss the curriculum and how they were finding it and seeing exactly what they have learned, it *is* very different than daycare and they have learned a lot more than I did at a comparable age. In September 2009 François entered his fourth year of schooling still at the ripe old of age of five. Wow!

Alex

François started school a whole two years before I did. Back before all the drama of PS Fab, PS Just OK and sleepless nights, we had our first round of craziness in the name of education with preschool. When F-Bomb was not quite three, we had just been through the first round of private pre-school applications, and he had been wait-listed everywhere. We kept in contact with the director of admissions at our top choice and spoke to her every month or so. It was she who remembered that she'd just heard of a new preschool that had a drop-out situation and had one opening for a three-year-old boy. Simon jumped off the phone with her, called me and I immediately called the school. I raced over with a checkbook and filled out an application on the spot. François had a great year there, and we were thrilled that two years later when it came time to apply for Johan, he was considered a sibling legacy. It didn't hit me until I heard other parents obsessing over whether they'd heard back from our school that we were very lucky that the J-Boy was a legacy. Johan, like his brother, spent his year doing art studies on Pollock, Miro and Van Gogh, watched caterpillars turn into butterflies, made more than one shark puppet and proudly brought home a potted marigold for Mother's Day. With so many school choices in the city, do you have to pick one school for all kids in your family? Not necessarily, but it helps. At the preschool level, I firmly believe that one school is as good as another for both kids, even though they have their differences. One thing I heartily recommend is choosing a school that's as close to your home as possible. I still can't believe we applied to a pre-school on the Upper West Side of Manhattan the first year. We'd have been killing ourselves and each other by the end of the year. Early childhood development and feeder schools be damned. I really, truly believe that where you went to pre-school simply does not matter when it comes time to apply to Northwestern or Yale. That's my story and I'm sticking to it.

Throughout the entire school application process, there have been many, many interviews. Interviews with par-ents. Interviews with children. Interviews with caregivers. Normally schools don't interview the babysitter, but during an interview with one of the boys, I came out to find an admissions associate chatting away with our nanny about his motor skills. There are playgroups with 10 children where the kids engage in "observed free play" while the teachers take notes in the corner and the parents pace the hallway outside in a controlled panic. All those interviews were to determine whether or not the boys were accepted to school, but even once we got into PS Fab, there were still interviews to be endured. The class grouping interview was new for our fam-ily with Johan, since François entered PS Fab after the year had started and went into the only class that had a space. Our J-Boy was accepted to school and asked to turn up at an intake interview. I'm guessing that with multiple classrooms they didn't want all the rambunctious kids or the kids who needed extra help or the kids with irritating parents all in one class. During his interview Johan was calm, cool, collected and absolutely uninterested in the work the teacher had for him. He quickly drew the picture she asked and got up to check out the farm animal toys nearby. She quickly followed him and picked up a cow. "Is this a dog?" she asked. He literally winked at her and said, "No, it's a cow." After 30 minutes of farm animal discussion, the evaluation was over. Of course I obsessed a little on the way home—did they think he couldn't concentrate? Was the work they asked of him too easy? Too difficult? Am I going absolutely nuts and do I need a slap 'round the ears? Maybe.

Something that was never an issue for us, but became one after we put our lives on TV, was raising our children with more than one language in the house. Simon and I feel it's very important to teach kids the skill of learning languages and communicating in more than one. We decided it didn't really matter which language we chose, but if the kids grew up being able to learn other languages and speak more than one, they'd have an easier time learning additional languages later on. We chose French as that's the one language other than English that Simon and I are both pretty strong in. It has nothing whatsoever to do with the choice of François' first name—he is named after Simon's father, a Dutchman born in Belgium. We started speaking to François using both languages shortly after birth. Once we joined the au pair program, we hired au pairs who were native French speakers. Native is the most important word in that phrase; one year we had a European au pair who wasn't French and didn't speak it fluently enough to communicate well with the boys. At any rate, our goal was that our au pair would speak only French to the boys and we would speak only English, except when in French-speaking countries, then no English at all. We stuck to this most of the time during our years with au pairs. Our current nanny, however, doesn't speak French. We speak French some of the time to the boys, and always at bedtime. During preschool, Johan attended a full-immersion program one day per week and his French quickly surpassed François'. Johan also seemed more interested in the language to begin with. François began to see speaking French as a competition with his brother—after dragging his heels for what seemed like forever, he asked us repeatedly to put him in a French after-school program, which we did the following fall. These days they enjoy a once-a-week program after school. Do they speak it fluently? No, and to be honest neither do we—we get by but certainly don't speak like someone who lives in a French-speaking country. Can they communicate on the playground in St. Barths without throwing a tantrum, and order what they want in a restaurant? Usually, yes. Do they understand that people in different countries speak different languages and learning more than one is a good skill? Absolutely 100 percent yes.

What else? I believe in not being condescending to children. I've always been touchy about respect for one's intelligence, and remember clearly being five or six years old and livid over the fact that some adult was treating me like an idiot. We've always tried to give our children as much information as they can handle, without bombarding them. You can't speak to a child like an adult; it goes over their heads. On the other hand, we try not to dumb down the concept, just speak slowly and use words they understand. When Simon's stepfather died, we explained to them what cancer was. Part of this was televised, but the off-camera part involved a constant stream of conversation over a month. What is cancer? Can you catch it? Does it always kill people who get it? Does it hurt?

As a former actor, I've always gotten into play-acting and dressing up with my children. Perhaps a little too much. But I've taken the opportunity to show off a few old monologues, complete with bounding around like a puppy. If you have knowledge, why not share it? If you happen to know Puck's speeches from a *Midsummer Night's Dream* by heart with tumbling and staged sword play, why the heck don't you share that with your boisterous boys, who love it and run around shouting, "Thou speakest aright!" Perhaps that idea doesn't work in every situation—I wouldn't bother teaching them how to beg for more gruel like Oliver Twist or pick a pocket like Fagin, but most things are worth passing on.

Simon
Alex and I both love to make up silly songs and rhymes, and have also done quite a bit of that with the kids. We wanted them to know their names and how to spell them early on, and along with the ABCs would sing these to them: "F-R-

A-N-Ç-O-I-S, F comes first and R is next, F-R-A-N-Ç-O-I-S, François, François. And J-O-H-A-N, J comes first and O is second, J-O-H-A-N, Johan, Johan." Without me standing over you singing it annoyingly into your ear it's probably hard to appreciate, but it was a little sing-songy tune that the boys immediately picked up.

TOP 10 FAVORITE "DEVELOPMENTAL" THINGS TO DO:

10. Translate simple songs into other languages. We sing them Twinkle Twinkle Little Star in English, French and Latin. Frere Jacques in French, English and Dutch, etc.

9. In the car, ask, "What can you see that you've never seen before?" In NYC, there's always something. Discuss.

8. Parental delaying tactic: If they want something that you want to delay giving them, make them ask in every language they can before giving in.

7. Make a guessing game out of them asking for something. Don't tell me what it is, but, "It's red. It's a food. It's got a stem and it's in the bowl with the bananas."

---

6. Math games. All the time. Another good delaying tactic is to make kids "pay" for whatever they're hassling us for. Example— Johan wants a cookie, and I tell him it costs two dimes. He goes to the toy cash register and retrieves two play dimes, brings them over and gets his cookie.

5. Almost every parent at some time or another needs to park the kids in front of the TV. Sometimes they want a DVD and have seen every title they own five times. I put it on in another language and have them see if they can decipher their favorite superhero movie in French or Spanish. Reminds me of living in Italy and improving my comprehension by watching dubbed versions of *Back to the Future* and *Point Break.*

4. François sometimes gets frustrated with the simple 100-word books he has to read for homework, but one day he perked right up when we suggested he read them to Johan.

3. If one kid needs a time-out, usually a minute for each year of their age, we might have the other boy time-keep (i.e., count to 60 four times for Johan or six times for François).

2. Interview the kids about the rest of the family. I love to ask Johan what he thinks of François, the cats, Daddy, me. His juices get flowing and he always comes up with really creative stories.

1. Stoke their memories. I asked François if he could remember the last time I cried, and he said, "Yes, you cried when you'd been in Ohio for work and when you came home I told you Daddy was sick and I took care of him. You cried like a baby!" He remembered this nine months after it happened, and it blew my mind. Kids remember so much, and I love asking them about it.

Chapter 13

Urban Wonderland

Taking Advantage of Raising a Child in the Urban Jungle

Look, Mommy, that man has a big snake around his neck!

Sure enough, the 20-something guy walking past us had a huge yellow and white python wrapped around his neck and upper torso.

Mommy, there's the man who sings on TV! He has children, too!

One thing specific to NYC and our neighborhood is that many of the children's musicians whose videos run on PBS Kids, Nick Jr. or the Disney Channel actually live within a few blocks of us and we see them in the park or on the street with their own children, which is another opportunity for education. Both our boys know that although they've seen Dan Zanes on television many a time and listen to his CDs often, it's not OK to leap on him in the street with hugs and kisses (unless it's Halloween and he has a pumpkin on his head).

Can we go into that shop? That dress in the window is beautiful and you should wear it. And you need a bracelet and a necklace, too.

Both boys have inherited our shopping genes. Part of the walking culture of New York City is that shops are easily accessible by young ones, and storeowners know this very well. We allow the boys to window shop, and it becomes a treat when they are well behaved enough to go inside.

What language is that lady singing? It's not English or French.

Raising children with more than one language in their ears can be frustrating, particularly when they go through phases where they say, "We're in America, speak English." However, we were ecstatic once, when listening to a song on the radio in German, that François recognized that the language was not English or French but something else entirely. Our boys know that people in different countries have different words for the same things, and that many people from all over the world come to live in New York City and speak English plus the language they grew up with in their home country and maybe a few others.

The Brooklyn Bridge is playing hide and seek!

Living in New York City, we see some of its more spectacular sights regularly if not every day, like the Brooklyn Bridge, the Statue of Liberty and the Empire State Building. The boys were fascinated one morning when, while driving on the BQE in Brooklyn, we could only see part of the Bridge due to heavy fog. A headless Statue of Liberty always provokes a reaction as well!

Because we're in the middle of it, our children are learning so much since merely navigating the city is a teaching tool. In every neighborhood, different cultures exist, often quite visually distinct from their own. Why is that man wearing a big fur hat with long curls and a white shawl? He's Hasidic, one of the most observant forms of Orthodox Judaism. Why is there a big paper dragon on the street with people in it? Because it's the Chinese New Year and we're in Chinatown. Why are all the people on our street shouting in French and throwing things? Do they need a reason for that? Oh, actually it's Bastille Day. Why is that lady squatting between two parked cars? Ummmmm, let's not discuss that one. Aren't we running late?

Whether it's the Macy's Thanksgiving Parade, planting trees in the park for Earth Day, the craziness of Halloween, the lighting of the Christmas tree in Rockefeller Center or the shortened performances at the opera translated into English for the young ones during school vacations, urban areas are magical places to raise children during the holidays. At school they get to participate in pretty much every major holiday ritual, and the streets are decorated, depending on the neighborhood, for Christmas, Hanukkah, Memorial Day… you name it.

Urban Wonderland

Mummies and Werewolves at Halloween

Winter Snowman with Ice Cream

187

We count ourselves lucky every day that we live in New York City, one of the richest cultural resources a parent could hope for. As long as you can make it out the front door, most days you are bound to see something you've never seen before. If we had the time and ability, we could do something different every day—although because of the diversity, simply stepping outside the house can be different. There's always someplace to go on a rainy day, whether it's a children's museum, a bookstore or simply the enormous Ferris Wheel in the toy store. Even riding the subway is fun for a kid, regardless of the destination.

Yes, there are downsides to living in a large urban area— you have to really work to see animals (live ones that is), and there are no big pastures outside Central or Prospect Park. However, we don't really live in a concrete maze. Our neighborhood is full of townhouses with leafy backyards, and trees line every street. We know everyone on our block and even have dinner parties with neighbors occasionally. For the most part, the shops on our main streets are privately owned, usually by a young and hip or old-school family. A Dunkin' Donuts or a Starbucks may sneak in occasionally, but they coexist with the smaller establishments without choking them out, which is important. We were very lucky to find a townhouse in a great school zone, near literally hundreds of amenities in walking distance. Having lived within 50 feet of a 24-hour gourmet deli, I don't think I could ever go back. I came to New York because I thought it was the center of the universe and wanted to be in the middle of it all. Why shouldn't my children have the same experience? We're not living in Times Square—and one could argue that you don't get any real picture of New York there anyway, particularly with all the bizarre chain restaurants that have sprung up there during the Giuliani years. I like being able to get a plate of moules frites at 2 a.m. if I want, a Middle Eastern supermarket with every type of sugar-free, dried fruit you can imagine, hundreds of world-renowned landmarks within an easy commute and seeing the boys' moods improve in an instant when we happen to be stuck in slow traffic on the FDR and they unexpectedly get to watch a seaplane taking off from the East River.

Another upshot of living in an urban environment is that while people make fun of our kids' names as being unusual, the cultural diversity of New York ensures that there will always be many other interesting names, too.

Simon

When our names first became known across the country many people were shocked that a couple with Anglicized Biblical names, Alex(andra) and Simon, could name their children François and Johan. Accusations that we were trying to be European and pretentious could be refuted, if we bothered, by informing people that they were so-named after their paternal grandfather. (The fact that I had a foreign sounding last name, van Kempen, was always overlooked.) A common theme with too many of these comments was the prediction that in time our boys would be beaten up in the schoolyard due to having names like theirs, regardless of the family origin of the names. While realizing that those ignorant enough to make such accusations are exactly the ones who WOULD punch a kid due to his name, I also laughed at them as they clearly have no idea what it is like to live in New York City. I wonder which of the following kids, with whom François or Johan have shared a school classroom, will be doing the beating: Ombeline, Divesh, Laweeza, Frederique, Taha, Wilhelm, Cosmo, etc., well, you get the idea. The great thing about New York City is that it is a world city, and frankly it's no surprise that the headquarters of the United Nations is based here. This city, more than just about any other on Earth, has peoples from all the countries of the world and actually in certain neighborhoods like ours there really is not one dominant culture. As you can see among their fellow students, François and Johan are just another two kids in the class. For those who still live in homogenized parts of the U.S. our sons names' might sound strange, but in NYC (and other large conurbations) they're no more strange than the rest of the kids sitting next to them in class, which is to say that their names aren't strange at all.

Alex
Quite right, in all their years of schooling neither boy has shared a classroom with a Tom, Jennifer, Sara or John. But even going beyond names, the microcosm that is New York City is fascinating to kids and adults.

During the holidays in New York we try to take the kids to see the decorations and sights, but don't like fighting the crowds at the same time. One New Year's Eve, we decided to drive around to see the holiday windows at Bendel's, Bergdorf's, Bloomingdales and other department stores, knowing that most tourists would be in Times Square awaiting the ball drop. As we passed St. Patrick's Cathedral on the way to Saks, the boys noticed that there were lots of police officers milling about outside, presumably waiting for midnight and watching for drunken people.

François: What are those?

Alex: Paddy wagons. (I kept my answer
              short, as I was trying to see where we
              could park to look at the windows.)

François: Why are they there?

Alex: To keep us safe.

François: From the church?

(Simon and I nearly died laughing over his innocent question.)

We share so much with our kids on a daily basis just going about the city, and when family comes in from out of town it's kind of thrilling (aren't we such good parents? … let's injure our hands patting ourselves on the back!) to hear our kids act as tour guides. When Johan pipes up to tell our visiting friend, "We're in Chinatown, where dumplings come from," we have to laugh. Whether it's a stroll down the Brooklyn Promenade, a visit to the Chrysler Building or the Central Park Zoo, it's amazing to see the pride they have in their city, even at a young age. They love New York as much as we do.

TOP 10 REASONS NEW YORK IS THE CENTER OF THE UNIVERSE TO A KID:

10. The ice cream factory at the Fulton Ferry Landing.

9. Standing in the middle of the walkway on the Brooklyn Bridge, screaming our heads off at the cars going under our feet.

8. Pausing at the entrance to a skyscraper and watching your child crane their neck all the way back, yet they still can't see the top of the building: "Daddy, does that building go all the way up to the moon?"

7. Coney Island.

6. Every weekend there's a street carnival in at least one neighborhood.

5. Instead of watching *Sesame Street* on TV, you can go and watch it being filmed.

4. There are more songs with NYC in their titles than any other city.

---

3. All the best superheroes live in Gotham City! "Mommy, where is Batman's house? In Manhattan or Brooklyn?"

2. There's a sense that anything is possible at any moment. I've never once heard our kids say something "can't be done."

1. If a kid says, "I live in New York," no further explanation is needed.

Chapter 14

"Daddy, a Cow! And It's Not in a Zoo!"

Getting Urban Kids Out of the City
and Into Greener Pastures

Simon

When Alex and I first broached the possibility that we'd have children together, after years of stating we wouldn't, the second thing I had to reconcile was that they were going to have a vastly different childhood than mine. All parents want their children to have advantages they lacked but apart from that, the biggest difference for me was that my childhood was just so different than theirs would be—not least being separated by four decades and 10,000 miles.

I was born in Brisbane, the capital city of the state of Queensland in Australia, which at that time had a population of just over 600,000 and when I was three we moved to a very small town in western New South Wales (NSW), Walgett, with a population of under 2,000, most of whom were Aborigines, Australia's indigenous peoples. Not long before my sixth birthday we moved again, 450 miles east to a small coastal town in northern NSW called Ballina. I remember as we drove in, as a family of six, we passed the town sign stating: *Ballina, NSW, Population 6,000.* My father suggested that one of us should jump out and change the final zero to a "6."

Simon, Age 5, in Walgett, Australia

We spent the next seven years there and it was a wonderful place for a young boy, aged from five years, 10 months to 13 to spend his preteen years. But just six weeks after we arrived I became fatherless, a situation that has probably affected me in more ways than I realize. I vividly remember being woken by Mum at around 6 a.m. one morning and being told that Dad had died during the night. Weirdly my first comment was to ask if I should go and wake my 10-year-old brother, who was still sleeping in our room. No, it wasn't necessary, she said. He needed to sleep, as he'd been up half the night helping Mum. The next few months honestly remain a blur in my memory; we returned to Brisbane for a short time and I went to school there for a few weeks before heading back to Ballina, although I have no idea why—the only tie to the area was that my father was buried there.

Throughout those years we lived in five different houses: Cherry Street, Norton Street, Skinner Street, Pine Avenue, East Ballina and finally North Creek Road. Ballina has a very temperate climate with lots of rain as well as many streams, farms and woods (and mischievously—golf courses, which I'll come to later!) for playing outdoors. Many a day I'd spend fishing tadpoles out of streams and brought them home in jars to watch them grow legs before releasing them when they were almost too big to fit in the jar. Or I would marvel at sugar cane burning time and at the many creatures that would race away from the burn off onto our rear lawn that abutted the sugar farm. I particularly remember picking up and carrying into the house one year what I thought was a little whip snake, a mildly poisonous snake, and watching my older brother freak out. In fact, I'd carried in Australia's most deadly snake, the brown. We promptly went outside and beheaded it. While my childhood might have been a financially hard one, it was certainly in these years an exciting one and in reality we lacked for very little. Sure we didn't have a color TV, but with only two channels available to us anyway and the great outdoors beckoning, it was much more fun to get on our bikes and go riding and exploring the outskirts of town. There were near misses I suppose as both my younger brother and I were befriended by this old guy, Dick, who lived on the outskirts of town in a small tin shed. I was 12 and Adam was 8, and Dick loved for us to come over to his home or shed and would give us cookies and take us on excursions to the town dump to look for useful things. (Today it has a trendy name "free-cycling," but then was called scavenging.) Many an afternoon during our long school summer vacation, Adam and I would spend with Dick and while things were never that inappropriate (he occasionally pulled out an early *Playboy* magazine back from the days when the lower regions were airbrushed out), I do remember hearing as a young adult one time when I was back visiting that there had been pretty strong rumors of pedophilia.

For those long summer months Dick would regale us about WWII, take us fishing or town dump scavenging and while he never ever became a surrogate father figure to me, I can't deny that there were times that being around an older man, even if he was old enough to be my grandfather, made me miss my own even more.

So the two biggest differences I foresaw for my boys was 1) I wanted to stay alive long enough to father them and 2) Ballina and New York City are two pretty different places.

The most obvious thing that inner city urban living

entails is that the majority of the population (and children) live in apartment buildings, particularly in high-density cities like NYC and Paris. We did for the first 22 months of François' life, but once Johan was on the way I was determined, as was Alex, to own our own bit of dirt. Alex once made a comment that became infamous about not wanting to live in the suburbs, and that's true for both of us, although it wasn't meant to appear as derogatory as it did. Buying our townhouse in Cobble Hill, not only allowed us to have a 22 by 40-foot backyard with a swing-set, blow-up pool in the summer as well as a concreted area for trikes and dirt to play in, but it also abuts and joins onto some 46 other backyards. This creates what I've read is called an "urban donut hole"—a mini oasis of trees and greenery flanked by buildings, which welcomes all sorts of animals throughout the year; squirrels are abundant. Recently a raccoon wandered into our house late one night. We have beautiful red cardinals, blue jays, the occasional woodpecker and a myriad of other birds I've yet to identify fly in.

It's not quite the same childhood that I experienced, but as the boys get older I certainly plan to get them out of the city more on weekends and see more of what's to offer within an hour's drive. Where François is well ahead of me at the same age is that on our various trips abroad he has observed (and scampered after) three lumbering iguanas, goats, chickens, camels, kangaroos, koalas, snorkeled chasing clownfish and so on. While these occasional trips are no replacement for living among such fauna on an everyday basis, these sightings mean that just because we live in a major metropolis they will

still get to go camping, fishing, pumpkin picking and maybe
even chicken plucking, like I did as a kid.

Alex
Camping, fishing and the chance to manhandle pump-
kins and chickens are all available in the Midwest. As
I mentioned earlier, one of the places I spent a lot of
time while growing up was in rural southeast Kansas
near my father's oil properties. One of my brothers still
lives there and we go back when we can to visit him and
friends. The fastest way to get there from New York is
to fly into Kansas City and drive about an hour south.
Once, minutes before our arrival, the boys were getting
a bit antsy. Aged two and four at the time, they were
bored and staring out the window at pastures on either
side of the winding two-lane highway. Suddenly, Johan
piped up, "Cow! Cow!" For a second I thought he was
saying, "Ow!" and had hurt himself, so I whirled around
and stared into the backseat expecting blood and tears,
or at least a scratch. I saw instead two boys transfixed
by a big black animal at the fence, almost in the ditch.
François chimed in, "That's not a zoo, that's a farm! Can
we go and milk the cows?" Although we didn't stop right
then and there, I think every kid should have the chance
to go fly-fishing with hip waders, milk a cow, pick berries
(and eat them) and dive into a brackish pond where their
feet get really muddy and gooey on the bottom. New
York has lots of excitement, but it does not offer the
opportunity to ride a kiddie quad bike down the center

of a residential street safely. We can pitch a tent in the backyard, but unless we download them onto the iPod, there are no bear noises.

As much as we love the city and everything it has to offer, we think it's important to balance that with opportunities to get out into big open areas where no one's around. That really does seem like the difference—it's very easy to take the kids to Central Park or Prospect Park and let them chase squirrels and tourists, but you still have loads of other humans around you. In rural areas we can let the boys ramble through a meadow and the only living things they'll see are birds, worms and ants. Although it takes a little legwork, there are plenty of options to be had outside the city. Some involve short drives or train rides away and others are a bit farther, but with young children, it really doesn't take much to change their reality for a weekend and allow them to experience something new. To a three-year-old, the difference between Brooklyn and East Hampton is almost as much as Earth to the Moon. We were aware that by choosing to raise our children in New York we would be thousands of miles away from our mothers and extended family. Going to Granny's house involves vacation time and an airplane trip versus a quick drive across town. So in our case, we discovered how important it is to build a "chosen family" in New York—friends to whom we would happily entrust our children and take care of theirs (or their pets).

Urban Giraffes in Sydney

Something I've noticed as an adult is that in busier cities, people tend to value what little vacation time they have that much more. Memorial Day weekend, for example, meant nothing more to me as a kid than a parade on Monday. As a grown-up living life at 100 miles per hour, this weekend has grown into an annual event involving a trip out of the city, activities for children and adults and a real breath of fresh air following a busy May. A great way to combine a break from the everyday with expanding your kids' horizons is to visit friends outside the city. For the last five years we've spent Memorial Day weekend in the Hamptons, either renting a house or staying with friends. Last year we stayed with friends who have a house with a large yard, a pool and tennis courts, all things we don't have in the city. The boys disappeared into the pool on Saturday morning, surfaced for a quick lunch and didn't return until bedtime. Our hosts had a metal detector and hid coins in the grass, which the boys happily hunted and found. To a five-year-old, a quarter can be a treasure!

Other trips we've made have been to visit high school and college friends, or relatives, who live in completely different parts of the country or other countries altogether. My aunt and uncle's Texas home has a beautiful outdoor kitchen, something that would never be feasible or practical in New York but is absolutely fascinating to the boys (and us for that matter). Though they live in the middle of Dallas, my cousins walked barefoot with the boys to the local park without any fear of things the bottoms of their feet might encounter. And although the Atlantic Ocean is way too cold for swimming off Long Island in the spring, it's nice and windy, which is perfect for flying kites on the beach. The boys' Australian cousins were mesmerized by François and Johan's casual ease at using the subway at home in New York, and when we visited them last year their then five-year-old cousin, Ties, gave a very succinct explanation of which snakes are OK to pick up and which ones "could make you die, so don't touch them."

If one were to psychoanalyze city dwellers' vacation choices, I think that there are two types of people who live in New York. Those who want to be in the center of the action at all times, and those who love action for the most part but also need to get away occasionally and do nothing, see no one and just breathe. That's why we like to travel to places during

202

low season, and another reason why the Hamptons in the summer is fun but can be tiring. Heading to the places like the Caribbean at the end of the season means we can take advantage of everything without having to wait in line or deal with extra people—it's a true social retreat.

Simon and I were both lucky to have experienced both rural and urban settings as children, and did worry a little bit about raising our two boys in the middle of one of the biggest cities in the world. While there are issues that may arise as they get older, we've so far been very happy with our choice.

TOP 10 DIFFERENCES WE'VE NOTICED BETWEEN CITY KIDS AND COUNTRY KIDS:

10. Country kids know their way around a toolshed. Our nephew may not be able to carry a heavy suitcase up our stoop when he visits, but he can stealthily swing open a 50-pound shed door in about 10 seconds, find an open box of matches and start lighting them.

9. Our two city kids don't know what to do with an unleashed dog. Despite being told to stay on his side of a fenced-in area where two dogs were roaming free, François jumped over to look at the doghouse and soon found himself pinned against the wall being licked to death by an overly friendly Labradoodle.

---

8.   Kids in the country don't run through tall grass without at least thinking about putting on shoes. Johan started to go tearing through a field and his 10-year-old cousin screamed, "Stop! Put on your snake boots!"

7.   Suburban kids know they'll get lost on the winding roads if they leave their driveway. Some of our visiting underage pals have commented how easy it is to get around New York City because "the streets are straight."

6.   City kids can get a cab faster than most grown-ups. Even jaded cab drivers think it's cute when a four-year-old screams, "Taxi!" from his father's shoulders.

5.   When country kids visit us in the city, they want to go to the 24-hour deli across the street five times a day. Why? Because it's there.

4.   In the country, gun safety involves going to classes, whereas in the city, it involves telling a police officer if you see one.

3.   When those same Aussie cousins visit NYC, the kids are shocked that we only drive the car about once a week. Which begs the question, why do we even have one?

2. City kids are used to being taken to all sorts of restaurants and quickly learn what to order in each. François used to complain loudly if taken out for Thai, until he learned to order Pad Thai with just noodles and sauce, no chicken.

1. Whether there are three kid-friendly activities available in a small town on any given day or 32 options in our neighborhood, you can count on all the kids to whine and say, "There's never anything to do!"

Chapter 15

You're Such a Great Parent, You Should Be on TV (LOL)

Parenting On-Screen vs. Off-Screen

Alex

I am the perfect mother. I am a fabulous diva in the house, my children and husband adore me and I can do no wrong. Look up "Mommylicious" in the dictionary and you will see a photo of me in a ball gown, breast-feeding an infant while making Osso Buco and directing carpenters to build a bookcase for my Dickens and Shakespeare. On the weekends, I mulch our organic garden with homemade compost, brush the cats, bake bread and amuse the boys by standing on my head singing the *Gilligan's Island* theme song in Latin. Simon sits on a hassock in the living room, cuddling the children while catching up on world events and the cricket score via all the international newspapers on his BlackBerry. Later in the afternoon he will mow the backyard, prune the hedges, change the oil in the car and rewire a few lamps while teaching the boys calculus. And if you believe that, please e-mail me your savings account information and password so I can wire you $10 million from the central bank of a developing country.

Simon

I am not sitting on a hassock in the living room, no ma'am. I am lurking in your closet trying on all those fabulous Cavalli ball gowns I convinced you to buy (me), while I add an "e" to the end of my first name and try to seduce every one of your friends' husbands… well, everyone except Mario, that is.

Alex

Surprisingly, I never questioned our parenting skills (much) before signing up for a reality show. That's not to say I thought we were fabulous, but we were doing just fine. Little did I know that once our family was on edited display, every little word and action would be picked apart by people who really have nothing better to do than criticize others. We didn't expect that the kids would look as hyper as they did in the first season of our show, but in hindsight we should have seen it coming. Do cute kids behaving themselves make good TV? Should you go on a reality show and bring your young family along if you've never watched the genre before? Maybe if we had we'd have run away screaming, or maybe we'd have still done it but been better prepared to be skewered the first year. As long as there are confident (naïve?) people in the world who don't watch TV, you will have a few of those same individuals willing to open up their homes to camera crews thinking, "What could possibly go wrong?"

Lights, Camera, Action!

Psychologists have said that the act of observing someone changes their behavior. Most reality TV participants say, "No, I don't behave any differently when the cameras are around. I am who I am!" Adults and teenagers are better at this than young kids. We are able to handle the idea that although there is a crew of people around, we are wearing body mics under our clothing and a big fuzzy boom is over our heads, we should attempt to ignore it all and behave as normally as possible. For kids, it's that much more difficult, and in those situations they can be really unpredictable. We work hard to keep it real when we're shooting and mostly it's easy, but not all the time, which is why many people who are very entertaining at parties wind up not making good reality TV subjects.

When people ask me how I could put such ill-mannered children on television, I laugh and tell them that our children never misbehave! They are perfectly articulate young gentlemen who shake hands, look people in the eye and have stimulating conversations about politics and health care reform with new acquaintances at cocktail parties. They love the TV crew and try to be helpful when moving camera equipment. They always put everything they touch back in its proper place and they never, ever fart on camera. Uh-huh.

Simon

After the first season aired I quickly realized that there was no successful way to rebut people attacking our parenting of our boys, based on the few minutes they'd seen on the show. Whether we had fallen into the trap of agreeing to film a "breakfast scene reading the morning paper" in late afternoon when the boys were definitely not in morning mode, or allowed them to stay up way past their bedtimes, the retort was always the same—you're bad parents because you do *a*, *b* or *c*, and if it wasn't that complaint, then it was, "You shouldn't put your children on TV."

Now three years in, I don't think that appearing on the show has harmed either boy. Yes, in subsequent seasons we were much more aware of situations to avoid with them on camera, but we have three years of great footage of them as young kids and they're learning some camera skills and confidence around other people. While they are still not yet at an age where the negative things people might write about them has any effect and we are all enjoying it, then we'll continue. If we or they have doubts over whether we should continue then we'll seriously think about stopping but that decision will be ours and not based on some anonymous comment or fly-by post.

Never Work with Children or Animals...

TOP 10 HILARIOUS THINGS THE BOYS HAVE DONE WHILE FILMING OR AT PHOTO SHOOTS:

10. *Credit or Debit?* In St. Barths, every year we take a mom and child(ren) photo on top of Pointe Colombier, the highest spot on the island. Three years ago, François didn't want to stand still and we were worried about him falling, as it is the edge of a cliff. Simon gave him a credit card to play with, and unintentionally it was his black AmEx. Monsieur François likes to play grocery store and all those things kids

do, and decided to swipe Alex's backside with the credit card. We have a couple of great photos (which will never see the light of day) of Alex laughing so hard she nearly dropped Johan while being on the receiving end of a metal credit card wedgie.

9.   *Kill the Burger, No, Really, Please Kill the Burger.* One of the more infamous kid scenes on our show involved François and a guest's boyfriend who arrived later and didn't particularly want to get involved in the grown-up drama. By then the younger kids had had enough and Simon and I just wanted to go home. François and his toy plastic kangaroo were drawn to the new guy in the room, a father of three. The end result? The kangaroo ate the burger, replayed endlessly from several angles. Viewers assumed the boyfriend was horrified and angered over the burger. I don't think he was thrilled, and neither were we, but it gave him something to do that didn't involve dealing with the other adults in the room.

8.   *Jellybeans Will Get You High.* If you're filming a scene and trying to keep the boys in their chairs, bribery is permissible. Any prize involving sugar, however, is a BAD idea. Just don't do it.

7. *Chocolate Looks Like Blood on TV.* There have been a few times that our chocoholic little boys have had treats while we're filming. I make homemade chocolate ice cream, and at my birthday celebration we had cupcakes. When filming season one, François came out with a chocolaty face and walked right in front of the camera. A crew member saw the extreme close-up and shouted, "Is he bleeding?" If you ever want to make a low-budget horror movie, stock up on chocolate syrup.

6. *When in Doubt, Bring Out a Three-Legged Dog.* Kids are naturally curious, and one of our more fun experiences involved filming with a handicapped dog. A house that we rented in the Hamptons two years ago came with the spa services of the owner, a masseuse, who brought with her a dog with three legs. The boys were fascinated by the animal and wanted to know how she could walk, why did she lose her leg, etc. I was so proud that the cameras caught them being politely inquisitive, which is truly real.

5. *Bored Now... Buh-Bye.* Although Johan is by far the wiliest, both boys often turn into escape artists when they've had enough shooting or waiting around. Whether it's at

home or out and about in the city, young kids don't like to sit still just out of shot. We don't have 24/7 childcare and when we're shooting at home on the weekends it's just the crew and us. After about 10 minutes, if we can't find the kids we check the crew van to see whether François has learned to drive yet, and how many toy boats and swords Johan has made out of that black aluminum foil they use for light filters. A bonus we hadn't counted on is that now that François is big enough for a body mic, the sound guys can hear what he's up to and track him. I can't wait until they mike up Johan, too!

4. *Confidence Will Get You Everywhere.* At a photo shoot, Johan was being fussed over by a group of stylists and makeup artists. Someone told him, "Johan, you are so cute!" Johan smiled and said in a complete deadpan, "I'm not cute. I'm *gorgeous.*"

3. *They Know How to Push Your Buttons.* We took the boys to a Christmas party in one of those over-the-top wonderland holiday stores where everything is gorgeous and expensive. While taking photos with Santa and his helpers, six-year-old François leaned over and whispered, "That elf is going to

get it." Needless to say I was on elf-watch for the rest of the party.

2.   *They Become Allies.* At a photo shoot with lots of children, one three-year-old girl had clearly had enough and wasn't cooperating. Johan started tickling her while François said to the photographer, "She needs a break or else she's going to start crying and that's going to stress me out."

1.   *When the Camera Rolls... François Rolls.* When François was four, we filmed a brunch in the Hamptons with friends of ours. It was late afternoon and hot, and the boys really wanted no part of sitting at the table and eating. It was painful for everyone involved. After we survived the meal, François took a walk with our friend Murray. Murray asked him how he liked filming, to which our little bugger replied, "Murray, when the camera rolls, *François rolls.*"

Chapter 16

The Light at the End of the Tunnel

Evidence of Self-Sufficiency

Alex

This is the chapter of hope. Sometimes when I want to jump off the Brooklyn Bridge because I think that the kids are never going to understand me, that things will never be easier, that they will wind up killing themselves before they can grow up to take on the city, something great will happen and I'll remember what we're working toward.

Right now we're in the trenches. We have young children who can be unreasonable, demanding, who relentlessly bug us and keep us from doing everything we want to do, or at least from doing it at the pace we'd prefer. There are many times when I've wanted to cry in frustration when it takes one and half hours to leave the house for the park (a five-block walk) due to capricious and exacting toddlers. If we can survive without killing them, however, there's a payoff that is already beginning to show itself.

One early weekend morning in August, after an unusually great night's sleep, I'm gently prodded awake by Simon, who suggests I boot up the computer and get some work done (I'd been complaining the day before that I wasn't being productive). The boys wake up as well, even though I'm being quiet as a mouse. They have a sixth sense for any sort of movement, I think. My best intention to work is then thwarted for half an hour until Simon mercifully takes the boys away for breakfast. In the interim I've managed to take my computer off the shelf and plug it in, put batteries into Operation and give a lesson in how to play it, remind the boys that they can't walk around with moon sand, diffuse two tantrums and answer all sorts of entertaining questions, such as, "Why can't I brush my private parts with my toothbrush? Why can I not color in the apple on the lid of your computer? Why doesn't Daddy like it when I scream in his ear?"

Sometimes answering illogical questions gets really, really frustrating. I'm the type of person who likes to tell someone to do something one time, explain where necessary and come back to see the task has been done. I don't like endless discussion, but with young children it's a way of life. Simon and I have to constantly check our frustration levels. In one 24-hour period while traveling with the family, I probably spent one full hour discussing why magic markers cannot be carried around with the caps off, particularly in a hotel suite with white couches and walls. You would think it's not necessary to explain that napkins on laps keep your clothes clean, but it does in fact take a spoonful of spaghetti spilled on a white shirt to drive that point home.

All Grown Up, So Far

Housekeeping with two exuberant young boys is like running an obstacle course uphill in the rain with one leg, a blindfold and heavy weights pulling at you. People with older children or no children used to look on the inside of our house in horror, and of course it was made worse by the fact that we bought a fixer-upper, which we renovated piece by piece. But seriously, who in their right mind would spend $10,000 on gorgeous sofas when kids will spill juice on them and jump up with their dirty shoes? As much as limestone bathroom vanities sound appealing, they would either be stained with toothpaste or assaulted by little fingers' attempts to remove the evidence in about 10 seconds. Prior to our renovation I made the decision that I would rather keep old furniture around that we don't particularly care about. Post-renovation, we tried to make our new purchases as environmentally friendly as possible, including eco-suede couches made out of recycled plastic bottles and repurposed wood. Regardless, I didn't buy anything that wouldn't react favorably to a Mr. Clean Magic Eraser Bath Scrubber, which I know is designed to rid of grime on tubs and toilets but often manages to sneak out of the bathroom and into our living room and other useful places. All our new furniture is easy to clean, as "green" as possible and great for use by messy, sticky, absolutely-lovable-even-when-they're-infuriating boys.

Children will beat you into submission with their needs. They are relentless, guilelessly calculating and will stop at absolutely nothing to keep you from doing whatever it is that you want to or need to do. Sometimes you really just want to get that pot off the stove while you're talking a client down off the cliff on your cell. At the same time you get to navigate an obstacle course of boys hanging on your legs, brandishing kitchen knives and the phone with which they want to call Grandma—conveniently forgetting that she is in Australia and it's 3 a.m. there. You want to get some work done on your computer? Expect that they'll stand over you, asking what you are doing and could they please draw something or type their names? And if you put on a DVD for them, they'll still request assistance pressing play, adjusting the volume and choosing the language.

Children can also turn you (temporarily) against your spouse. You want to sit quietly and finish your cocktail? Nope, it's your turn to run a lap around the restaurant's garden with the kids. You want to take a shower? Not a chance, I want to check my e-mail and tag photos on Facebook. I have had a really rough day at the office and I need you to feed the children, put them to bed and leave me alone while I try and shake off this day. For this reason I'm glad we stopped at two. A friend of mine from college and his partner adopted a boy who is about the same age as Johan, and he told me once that he and his partner would both get vasectomies if it were necessary to ensure that there would be no more children in their family. I think that this is where many relationships go sour—Simon and I are lucky that the frustration of navigating parenthood has brought us closer together rather than wedging us apart. When times are rough with the kids it's us against them, not each other.

Why would you ever have children if they are so profoundly irritating? While making you and your partner completely crazy, they are also the most lovable, delightful creatures in existence. How can you not look at the face of your three-year-old and be so happy you think your heart will burst when they say, "I love you, Mommy," or "Daddy is my best friend." We also remind ourselves how very, very lucky we are that we have two happy, healthy children. Life can change in an instant, and having a baby is not a guarantee of that baby growing into a child, a teenager or an adult. I felt that overwhelming sadness that seems like nausea when I heard that someone's newborn baby died, or that a fifth-grader in a local school was killed in a bicycle accident. Times like those you can feel guilty that you have two amazing kids who have no major allergies or illnesses and who love each other and love us. We are lucky and we know it. Let's go find a big piece of wood so I can knock on it.

They are alive, they are healthy and eventually they begin to "get it." Somehow you begin to see a light at the end of the tunnel when they start to demonstrate self-sufficiency.

I'm in the bathroom getting ready. I hear two-year-old Johan crying. Just as I'm about to stop and investigate, the crying stops. Four-year-old François comes running in:

Alex:	What happened?
François:	Johan was thirsty. I got up on the stepladder, got him a juice box and he's OK now.

When François severed his tendon and had to have surgery, Johan came into the recovery room with us to see him and sat on the end of the gurney as his brother came out from under sedation. When the nurse and Simon and I gently called to François, Johan sweetly sang out, "François, wake up!" When our big boy did open his eyes, he smiled at his little brother and I melted. Though they are certainly capable of pounding each other to a pulp, they also clearly love each other and are each other's best playmates. For this reason we're so glad we had two so close in age.

At 10 a.m. on a Sunday at home:

Alex:	Johan, will you tell me a story?
Johan:	OK. Once upon a time there was a boy called Johan. And he wasn't a baby, he was a boy. And he went to his mom's house, but his mom wasn't there, the wild things were. The one wild thing was Mommy, and the other wild thing was Daddy, and there was another wild thing that was François. And then they made pancakes and they ate them with chocolate chips inside. And then they ate gummy worms. And then they went to the park and they splattered some goo on us. Then we licked the goo and it was slime. Mommy, do you know that candy we had with slime? Where we dipped a stick into the salty thing and then into the goo? And Mommy, do you know we eat candy goo? Caaaaandy goooooo. Yum. OK, that's it.

After telling his story, Johan moved a little closer and half whispered conspiratorially... but not so low that Simon couldn't hear from across the kitchen.

221

Johan:	Mommy, may I have some cotton candy?
Simon:	No.
Johan:	No, I'm not asking you, I'm asking Mommy.
Simon:	Mommy's answer will be the same as mine.
Johan:	Ummm, Mommy, may I have some cotton candy?
Alex:	No.
Johan:	(Without missing a beat) OK, can I have some money?

After lunchtime, he got his cotton candy. No money changed hands.

After going through years of frustration over not being able to communicate with your little ones, feeling that they are personally invested in keeping you from doing what you want to do, etc., it's such an amazing feeling when you are able to share something you love doing, with the ones you love most. On a recent weekend away we were able to take our eldest, François, out snorkeling with us. Although he's not a terribly strong swimmer yet, he was able to wear the mask and snorkel and calm enough to float on top of the water balanced on my arm or Simon's back. It was absolutely magical to be able to show François all the fish and the undersea world, to show him why we love to scuba dive, and to experience his excitement and awe at seeing a school of 25 angel fish and 13 squid hovering near the rocks. Of course it helped that his second favorite movie is *Finding Nemo*, which he'd actually watched on French cable the night before. It was a beautifully clear day and he was ecstatic to see that this aquatic wonderland really existed. Although Johan was a bit too young to try it, he put on the mask and stuck his face into a six-inch deep reflecting pool in an enclosed area at the end of the beach. The only fish that make it into that area are smaller than our pet Japanese fighting fish at home, but he was properly amazed. "I'm scuba diving, François!" he crowed over and over.

TOP 10 MOMENTS OF "GETTING IT":

10. François held the door open for Mommy, making us realize he was big enough to physically do it.

9. Johan spontaneously answered a question in French—no prodding!

8. François stood over us while writing this book and began to read aloud over our shoulders.

---

7. The boys got themselves up on a Saturday morning, poured cereal and juice for themselves and only came in to jump on us at 9 a.m. The four of us snuggled for another hour without any crying, poking or fighting. That morning is up there with the best times in our lives as parents.

6. After taking the boys to see *Where the Wild Things Are*, François said, "The boy threw a tantrum, and then later a grown-up did, too. It wasn't OK for either of them to do that."

5. One hectic morning Alex made school lunches while Simon poured juice and coffee. We heard footsteps coming up the stairs and there were the boys. Dressed! Wearing shoes! Nothing needed to be changed or adjusted.

4. In the basement, Johan pointed to the Bugaboo stroller and said, "That's the Christmas tree holder." Well, that's all we use it for now!

3. At bedtime, at school drop-off and (usually) when babysitters arrive, there's no panic. The boys know that Mommy and Daddy are coming back.

2. Apropos of nothing, Johan said, "You give us time-outs because you are teaching us to be good grown-ups."

1. François made us both cry on his birthday when he said, "Thank you for having me."

Epilogue

On our journey of parenthood, we've realized that there is no "right way" to parent. We've made some seemingly obvious mistakes, but have also had some gratifying successes. When we sat down to write this book, I had a particular memory in my mind. The most comfort I have received from books, blogs and articles, has been from stories that make me feel better about what I'm doing, that we're not the only ones in this process. I hope while reading this that you've laughed knowingly, or even condescendingly, if it makes you feel better. I don't know why so many judgmental people expect perfection from children and parents, and it would be a happier world if more people would just take a deep breath and laugh. I remember reading a crazy story in Ayun Halliday's *The Big Rumpus* about choosing your battles and allowing a child to manhandle MetroCards picked up off subway platforms. I cracked up in relief, not that my kids have actually done that (well, that I know of) but that there were other mothers willing to admit that they weren't perfect.

Once I rode in a car with a good friend and her two children, nearly the same age as mine. The oldest was bored, annoyed, well and truly over being in the car and poking her brother, who didn't appreciate being used as a punching bag. The sassy sulkiness that ensued could easily have come from my children's mouths, and it hit me that we're all in this together.

Kid 1:	He's looking at me!
Kid 2:	No, I'm not! (Said looking right at her.)
Parent:	Uh-huh.
Kid 1:	He's torturing me!
Parent:	Really?
Kid 1:	I'm going to DIE!!!
Parent:	Before or after we get out of the car?

We joined a club called parenthood, either willingly or by accident, and each one of us is doing the best they can trying to raise our kids to become strong, useful members of society without losing their minds in the process. If you've made it to the end of this book, we salute you. If you are parents, we wish you happy, well-adjusted children who grow up to be competent adults who aren't in prison. We wish you grandchildren to spoil and slip extra candy to. We wish you all the amazing moments that happen, even when you're so frustrated you want to whack yourself or your partner in the head, when you take a deep breath and realize how much fun you're having. If you haven't had kids yet, or think you never will, we hope you take away that raising kids in a big city is magical, exciting and totally doable.

For more information about us, visit our website:
www.mccordvankempen.com

Acknowledgments

Without the assistance and inspiration of the following people and organizations, this book would not be what it is:

ALEX'S THANKS:
My best friend and husband, Simon. My inspirations and endless sources of material, François and Johan. Mom and Grandpa Bob for absolutely everything, Dad in spirit, David, Paul and all my family. To Elaine and all the vKs. To Coleen, Ety, Rosa and Anais. Brian, Ben, Nanette and the Artscetera gang, Sue and Becky, Bradley, Pascale, Patricia, Lauren, Merry, Kathy, Gwen and Melanie. The unsinkable Molly Talbot, Despina and Sava. It takes a village and you all live in it. Thank you so much. To Edward "Garou" Linders, thank you for your beautiful photos of the four of us. Thanks to Jason Allen Ashlock for believing in this project no matter what, and for leading us to the right publisher. Thanks to Rachel and Drew for being patient, and to Terese Kerrigan, Jamie Metrick, Nadina Persaud, Maryann Yin, Melissa Darcey and everyone at Sterling &

Ross Publishers. Thanks also go to Bravo and Shed Media. And thanks to Derek for being a cheerleader and to the cats for jumping on the keyboard and licking me without hitting "delete."

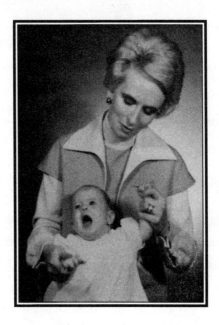

Alex, with Plenty to Say from the Beginning

SIMON'S THANKS:

Alex, as usual, has pretty much everyone covered. I do have to thank, from the bottom of my heart, my mother, who at 32 years of age found herself widowed with four children aged 13 months to 11 years. She managed through dedication, hard work and resolve to raise four well-adjusted, sane and sensible children, now all parents themselves.

This really is Alex's book with comments/paragraphs

here and there by me. She slaved over it (and me to get my bits written), but it is our book to the extent that without the four of us it would not and could not ever have happened. Now I know that sounds a little like I am stating the obvious, but what I really mean is that this book happened because Alex and I are largely in agreement about most things and have been like that for the 10 plus years we've been together. The great thing about us is that we have been in sync together for so long and while we are not quite the *two heads one body* that she suggested in the show's first season, we aren't that far away from being it. So my thanks go to Alex—for being online at 7 a.m. that Sunday morning in May 1999. Could you imagine where we'd be now if you hadn't been?

Beach Baby Simon